budget
food

budget
food

MURDOCH BOOKS

Contents

Soups

Chicken noodle soup

1.25 kg (2 lb 12 oz) chicken wings
2 celery stalks, chopped
1 carrot, chopped
1 onion, chopped
1 bay leaf
1 thyme sprig
4 flat-leaf (Italian) parsley sprigs
45 g (1½ oz) dried fine egg noodles
1 boneless, skinless chicken breast,
  finely chopped
snipped chives, to serve

Rinse the chicken wings and place in a large saucepan with the celery, carrot, onion, bay leaf, thyme, parsley, 1 teaspoon salt and 2 litres (68 fl oz/ 8 cups) water. Bring to the boil slowly, skimming the surface as required. Simmer, covered, for 1 hour. Allow to cool slightly. Strain and discard the chicken wings and the vegetables.

Cool the stock further, then cover and refrigerate for at least 1 hour, or until fat forms on the surface of the stock that can be skimmed off with a spoon.

Place the stock in a large saucepan and bring to the boil. Gently crush the noodles and add to the soup. Return to the boil and simmer for 8 minutes, or until tender. Add chopped chicken breast and simmer for 4–5 minutes, or until the chicken is cooked through. Serve topped with the chives.

Serves 4–6

Mushroom soup

2 tablespoons butter
1 onion, finely chopped
12 large (about 1.4 kg/3 lb 3 oz) field
  mushrooms, finely chopped
2 garlic cloves, crushed
2 tablespoons dry sherry
1 litre (35 fl oz/4 cups) chicken or
  vegetable stock
2 tablespoons flat-leaf (Italian) parsley,
  finely chopped
pouring cream

Melt the butter in a large saucepan and fry the onion until the onion is translucent but not browned.

Add mushroom and garlic; continue frying. Initially, the mushrooms may give off a lot of liquid, so keep frying until it is all absorbed back into the mixture. This will take 15–20 minutes.

Add sherry to the pan, turn up the heat and let the mixture bubble (this burns off the alcohol but retains the flavour). Cool slightly, then transfer to a blender and process until a smooth paste forms. Add the stock and blend until smooth. Add the parsley and a couple of tablespoons of cream and blend again. Pour mixture into the saucepan and heat gently.

Serves 4

Corn chowder

90 g (3¼ oz) unsalted butter
2 large onions, finely chopped
1 garlic clove, crushed
2 teaspoons cumin seeds
1 litre (35 fl oz/4 cups) vegetable stock
2 potatoes, peeled and chopped
250 g (9 oz/1 cup) tinned creamed
  corn
400 g (14 oz/2 cups) corn kernels
  (about 4 cobs)
3 tablespoons chopped parsley
125 g (4½ oz/1 cup) grated cheddar
  cheese
3 tablespoons pouring cream
  (optional)
2 tablespoons snipped chives
  (optional)

Melt the butter in a large heavy-based saucepan. Add the onion and sauté over medium–high heat for 5 minutes, or until golden.

Add the garlic and cumin seeds and cook for 1 minute, stirring constantly, then pour in the stock and bring to the boil. Add the potato, then reduce the heat and simmer for 10 minutes.

Add the creamed corn, corn kernels and parsley. Bring to the boil, reduce heat and simmer for 10 minutes.

Stir in the cheese and season to taste with sea salt and freshly ground black pepper. Stir in the cream, if using, and heat gently until cheese melts. Serve immediately, sprinkled with snipped chives, if using.

Serves 8

Chilled cucumber yoghurt soup

2 telegraph (long) cucumbers, about
    550 g (1 lb 4 oz)
1 large handful mint
2 garlic cloves, chopped
1 teaspoon dried mint
125 ml (4 fl oz/½ cup) milk
500 g (1 lb 2 oz/2 cups) Greek-style
    yoghurt
2–3 teaspoons lemon juice, to taste
3–4 drops Tabasco sauce, to taste
2 tablespoons finely snipped chives,
    to serve

Peel the cucumbers, halve them lengthways and scoop out the seeds. Set aside about one-third of one of the cucumbers.

Put the remaining cucumber in a small processor fitted with the metal blade. Add mint, garlic, dried mint and milk and process in short bursts for about 20 seconds. Add yoghurt, lemon juice, and Tabasco sauce to taste. Season well with salt and freshly ground black pepper. Blend until well combined and smooth, then transfer the soup to a bowl, cover and refrigerate for at least 2 hours to allow flavours to develop.

Finely dice the reserved cucumber. Ladle the soup into bowls and top with the diced cucumber and chives.

Serves 4

Note: The soup should be eaten within 1 day. It is not suitable for freezing.

Pasta and bean soup

200 g (7 oz) dried borlotti (cranberry)
  beans (see Note for option)
60 ml (2 fl oz/¼ cup) olive oil
90 g (3¼ oz) piece pancetta, finely
  diced
1 onion, finely chopped
2 garlic cloves, crushed
1 celery stalk, thinly sliced
1 carrot, diced
1 bay leaf
1 rosemary sprig
1 flat-leaf (Italian) parsley sprig
400 g (14 oz) tin chopped tomatoes,
  drained
1.6 litres (56 fl oz/6 cups) vegetable
  stock
2 tablespoons finely chopped flat-leaf
  (Italian) parsley
150 g (5½ oz) ditalini or other small
  dried pasta
extra virgin olive oil, to serve
grated parmesan cheese, to serve

Place the beans in a large bowl, cover
with cold water and soak overnight.
Drain and rinse.

Heat the oil in a large saucepan, add
the pancetta, onion, garlic, celery and
carrot, and cook over medium heat
for 5 minutes, or until golden. Season.
Add the bay leaf, rosemary, parsley
sprig, tomato, stock and beans. Bring
to the boil. Reduce heat and simmer
for 1½ hours, or until tender. Add
boiling water, if needed.

Discard the bay leaf, rosemary and
parsley. Scoop out 250 ml (9 fl oz/
1 cup) of the mixture and purée in a
food processor. Return to the pan,
season, and add chopped parsley and
pasta. Simmer for 6 minutes, or until
al dente. Remove from heat and set
aside for 10 minutes. Serve drizzled
with olive oil, sprinkled with parmesan
and pepper, if desired.

Serves 4

Note: You can use three 400 g (14 oz)
tins drained borlotti beans. Simmer
with vegetables for 30 minutes.

Beef and beet borscht

2 tablespoons olive oil
1 onion, chopped
2 garlic cloves, crushed
500 g (1 lb 2 oz) beef chuck steak, cut
   into 2 cm (3/4 inch) chunks
1 litre (35 fl oz/4 cups) beef stock
2 small beetroot (beets), scrubbed
   and trimmed
200 g (7 oz) tinned chopped tomatoes
1 carrot, cut into 1 cm (1/2 inch) cubes
2 potatoes, peeled and cut into 1 cm
   (1/2 inch) cubes
190 g (6 3/4 oz/2 1/2 cups) finely
   shredded cabbage
2 teaspoons lemon juice
2 teaspoons sugar
2 tablespoons chopped flat-leaf
   (Italian) parsley
2 tablespoons chopped dill
4 tablespoons sour cream
crusty bread, to serve

Preheat the oven to 200°C (400°F/
Gas 6). Heat the olive oil in a large
saucepan, add the onion and garlic
and sauté over medium heat for
5 minutes. Add the beef, stock and
1 litre (35 fl oz/4 cups) water. Bring
to the boil, then reduce the heat and
simmer, covered, for 1 1/4 hours, or
until the meat is tender. Remove the
meat, reserving the stock mixture.

Meanwhile, wrap each beetroot in foil
and bake for 30–40 minutes, or until
tender. Remove the foil and set aside
to cool, then peel and cut into 1 cm
(1/2 inch) pieces (wear rubber gloves to
stop the chilli staining your hands).

Return the stock to the boil. Add the
tomato, carrot and potato and season
with sea salt. Cook over medium heat
for 10 minutes, or until the vegetables
are tender. Add cabbage and cook
for 5 minutes. Return meat to the pan
with beetroot, lemon juice, sugar and
1 1/2 tablespoons each of the parsley
and dill. Cook for 2 minutes, or until
heated through. Season to taste and
divide the borscht among warmed
bowls. Top with a little sour cream,
sprinkle with the remaining chopped
herbs and serve with crusty bread.

Serves 4

Roasted tomato, almond and basil soup

60 ml (2 fl oz/¼ cup) olive oil
1 kg (2 lb 4 oz) large, vine-ripened
   tomatoes
1 large onion, finely chopped
2 garlic cloves, thinly sliced
50 g (1¾ oz/⅓ cup) blanched
   almonds, roughly chopped
2 handfuls basil, roughly torn
750 ml (26 fl oz/3 cups) chicken stock

Preheat the oven to 180°C (350°F/ Gas 4). Grease a baking tray with 1 tablespoon oil. Cut tomatoes in half, scoop out the seeds and arrange, cut side down, on the prepared tray. Roast for 15 minutes, then remove from the oven and set aside until the tomatoes are cool enough to handle. Discard the tomato skin and roughly chop the flesh.

Heat remaining oil in a large saucepan over medium–low heat. Gently sauté the onion and garlic for 5–6 minutes, or until soft and translucent. Add the chopped tomato, almonds and half the basil. Fry, stirring once or twice, for 5 minutes.

Transfer mixture to a small processor with a metal blade and process for 20 seconds, or until thick and smooth.

Return the mixture to the saucepan, stir in the stock and bring to the boil over medium–high heat. Stir in the remaining basil, season with salt and freshly ground black pepper, to taste, and serve immediately.

Serves 4

Creamy spinach and chicken soup

1 tablespoon oil
1 kg (2 lb 4 oz) chicken pieces
1 carrot, chopped
2 celery stalks, chopped
1 onion, chopped
6 black peppercorns
2 garlic cloves, chopped
bouquet garni (herbs of your choice
   bundled together and tied with string
   ie parsley, sage, thyme)
800 g (1 lb 12 oz) sweet potato,
   chopped
500 g (1 lb 2 oz) English spinach
125 ml (4 fl oz/½ cup) cream

Heat the oil in a large saucepan, add the chicken pieces in batches and brown well. Drain on paper towels. Pour off the excess fat, leaving only 1 tablespoon in the pan. Return the chicken to the pan with the carrot, celery, onion, peppercorns, garlic, bouquet garni and pour in 1.5 litres (52 fl oz/6 cups) of water.

Bring soup to the boil, reduce heat and simmer for 40 minutes. Strain, discarding vegetables, peppercorns and bouquet garni. Return the stock to the pan. Pull chicken meat from the bones, shred and set aside.

Add sweet potato to the stock in the pan. Bring to the boil, then reduce the heat and simmer until tender. Add the spinach leaves and cook until wilted. Process the spinach in batches in a food processor until finely chopped.

Return the spinach to the pan, add the shredded chicken and stir in the cream. Season to taste. Reheat gently before serving but do not allow the soup to boil.

Serves 6

Chunky vegetable soup

100 g (3½ oz/½ cup) dried red kidney
    beans or borlotti (cranberry) beans
    (see Note)
1 tablespoon olive oil
1 leek, halved lengthways, chopped
1 small onion, diced
2 carrots, chopped
2 celery stalks, chopped
1 large zucchini (courgette), chopped
1 tablespoon tomato paste
    (concentrated purée)
1 litre (35 fl oz/4 cups) vegetable stock
400 g (14 oz) pumpkin (winter
    squash), cut into 2.5 cm (1 inch)
    cubes
2 potatoes, cut into 2 cm (¾ inch)
    cubes
crusty wholemeal bread, to serve

Put the beans in a large bowl, cover with cold water and soak overnight. Rinse, then transfer to a saucepan, cover with cold water and cook on medium–high for 45 minutes, or until just tender. Drain and set aside.

Meanwhile, heat the oil in a large saucepan, add leek and onion, and cook over medium heat for 3 minutes without browning, or until they start to soften. Add the carrot, celery and zucchini, and cook for 3–4 minutes. Add the tomato paste and stir for a further 1 minute. Pour in the stock and 1.25 litres (44 fl oz/5 cups) water, and bring to the boil. Reduce the heat to low and simmer for 20 minutes.

Add the pumpkin, potato and beans, and simmer on low–medium heat for a further 20 minutes, or until the vegetables are tender and the beans are cooked. Season to taste. Serve immediately with crusty bread.

Serves 6

Note: To save time, use a 400 g (14 oz) tin red kidney beans instead of dried beans. Rinse well. There will then be no need to complete step 1.

Creamy brussels sprout and leek soup

1 tablespoon olive oil
2 rindless bacon slices, chopped
2 garlic cloves, chopped
3 leeks, white part only, sliced
300 g (10½ oz) brussels sprouts,
  roughly chopped
750 ml (26 fl oz/3 cups) chicken
  stock or vegetable stock
185 ml (6 fl oz/¾ cup) pouring cream
  or milk
slices of toasted crusty bread,
  to serve

Heat the oil in a large saucepan over medium heat. Add chopped bacon and fry for 3 minutes. Add the garlic and leek, cover and fry, stirring often, for a further 5 minutes. Add brussels sprouts, stir to combine, cover and cook, stirring often, for 5 minutes.

Add the stock and season with salt and freshly ground black pepper. Bring to the boil, then reduce heat, cover pan and simmer for 10 minutes, or until vegetables are very tender. Set aside to cool for 10 minutes.

Using an immersion blender fitted with a chopping blade, whizz the soup for 25–30 seconds, or until puréed. Stir through the cream or milk and gently reheat the soup. Serve with slices of toasted crusty bread.

Serves 4

Tip: For a vegetarian version of this soup, simply omit the bacon and use vegetable stock rather than chicken stock.

Mulligatawny

30 g (1 oz) butter
375 g (13 oz) chicken thigh cutlets,
  skin and fat removed
1 large onion, finely chopped
1 apple, peeled, cored and diced
1 tablespoon curry paste
2 tablespoons plain (all-purpose) flour
750 ml (26 fl oz/3 cups) chicken stock
50 g (1¾ oz/¼ cup) basmati rice
1 tablespoon chutney
1 tablespoon lemon juice
60 ml (2 fl oz/¼ cup) pouring cream

Gently heat butter in a large heavy-based saucepan. Cook the chicken on medium–high heat for 5 minutes, or until browned, then remove and set aside. Add onion, apple and curry paste to the pan. Cook for 5 minutes, or until the onion is soft. Stir in the flour and cook for 2 minutes. Add half the stock. Continue stirring until the mixture boils and thickens.

Return chicken to pan with remaining stock. Stir until boiling, then reduce heat, cover and simmer for 1 hour. Add rice for the last 15 minutes of cooking time.

Remove the chicken from the pan and remove the meat from the bones. Shred and return to the pan. Add the chutney, lemon juice and cream, and season to taste.

Serves 4

Spiced pumpkin and lentil soup

1 kg (2 lb 4 oz) pumpkin (winter
  squash)
2 tablespoons olive oil
1 large onion, chopped
3 garlic cloves, chopped
1 teaspoon ground turmeric
1/2 teaspoon ground coriander
1/2 teaspoon ground cumin
1/2 teaspoon chilli flakes
135 g (4 3/4 oz/1/2 cup) red lentils,
  rinsed and drained
1 litre (35 fl oz/4 cups) boiling water
90 g (3 1/4 oz/1/3 cup) plain yoghurt,
  to serve

Peel, seed and cube the pumpkin to give 700 g (1 lb 9 oz/4 1/2 cups) of flesh.

Heat the oil in a large saucepan over medium heat. Add the onion and garlic and fry for 5 minutes, or until softened, being careful not to burn the garlic. Add turmeric, coriander, cumin and chilli flakes and fry, stirring constantly, for 2 minutes.

Add the pumpkin, red lentils and boiling water. Bring to the boil, then reduce the heat and simmer, covered, for 20 minutes, or until the pumpkin and lentils are tender. Set aside to cool for 5 minutes.

Using an immersion blender fitted with a chopping blade, whizz soup for 30 seconds, or until evenly blended. Season with salt and freshly ground black pepper and reheat.

Ladle soup into four bowls, top with a spoonful of the yoghurt and sprinkle with freshly ground black pepper.

Serves 4

Mexican bean chowder

155 g (5½ oz/¾ cup) dried red kidney
    beans
165 g (5¾ oz/¾ cup) dried Mexican
    black beans (see Note)
1 tablespoon oil
1 onion, chopped
2 garlic cloves, crushed
½–1 teaspoon chilli powder
1 tablespoon ground cumin
2 teaspoons ground coriander
2 x 400 g (14 oz) tins chopped
    tomatoes
750 ml (26 fl oz/3 cups) vegetable
    stock
1 red capsicum (pepper), chopped
1 green capsicum (pepper), chopped
440 g (15½ oz) tin corn kernels
2 tablespoons tomato paste
    (concentrated purée)
grated cheddar cheese, to serve
sour cream, to serve

Soak kidney beans and black beans in separate bowls in plenty of cold water overnight. Drain. Place both beans in a large saucepan, cover with water and bring to the boil. Reduce the heat and simmer for 45 minutes, or until tender. Drain.

Heat oil in a large saucepan, add the onion and cook over medium heat until soft. Add the garlic, chilli powder, cumin and coriander. Cook for 1 minute. Stir in tomato, stock, capsicum, corn and tomato paste. Cook, covered, for 25–30 minutes. Add beans in the last 10 minutes of cooking. Stir occasionally.

Serve topped with the grated cheddar and a spoonful of sour cream.

Serves 6

Note: Mexican black beans are also known as black turtle beans.

Spicy chicken broth with coriander pasta

350 g (12 oz) boneless, skinless
  chicken thighs or wings
2 carrots, finely chopped
2 celery stalks, finely chopped
2 small leeks, finely chopped
3 egg whites
1.5 litres (52 fl oz/6 cups) chicken
  stock
Tabasco sauce

Coriander pasta
60 g (2¼ oz/½ cup) plain (all-purpose)
  flour
1 egg
½ teaspoon sesame oil
1 large handful coriander (cilantro)
  leaves

Put the chicken and vegetables in a large saucepan and push the chicken to one side. Add the egg whites to the vegetables. Using a wire whisk, beat until frothy. Warm the stock in another saucepan, then add gradually to the first pan, whisking constantly to froth the egg whites. Continue whisking while slowly bringing to the boil. Make a hole in the froth with a spoon and simmer, uncovered, for 30 minutes without stirring. Line a strainer with a damp tea towel (dish towel) and strain the broth into a bowl. Discard chicken and vegetables. Season well with salt, pepper and Tabasco.

To make the coriander pasta, sift the flour into a bowl and make a well in the centre. Whisk the egg and oil together and pour into the well. Mix to a soft dough and knead on a floured surface for 2 minutes, or until smooth. Divide the dough into four portions. Roll one portion out very thinly (best to use a pasta machine) and cover with a layer of evenly spaced coriander. Roll out another portion of pasta and lay this on top of the leaves. Repeat with the remaining pasta and coriander.

Cut squares of pasta around the coriander leaves. Bring the chicken broth to a gentle simmer. Add the pasta, cook for 1 minute and serve.

Serves 4

Smoked haddock chowder

500 g (1 lb 2 oz) smoked haddock
1 potato, diced
1 celery stalk, diced
1 onion, finely chopped
50 g (1¾ oz) butter
1 bacon slice, rind removed, finely
  chopped
2 tablespoons plain (all-purpose) flour
½ teaspoon mustard powder
½ teaspoon worcestershire sauce
250 ml (9 fl oz/1 cup) full-cream
  (whole) milk
2 very large handfuls chopped flat-leaf
  (Italian) parsley
60 ml (2 fl oz/¼ cup) pouring cream

To make the fish stock, put the fish in a frying pan (skillet), cover with water and bring to the boil. Reduce the heat and simmer for 8 minutes, or until the fish flakes easily. Drain, reserving the fish stock, then peel, bone and flake the fish.

Place the potato, celery and onion in a medium saucepan, and pour in enough of the reserved fish stock to cover them. Bring to the boil, reduce the heat and simmer for 8 minutes, or until vegetables are tender.

Melt the butter in a large saucepan over low heat. Increase heat to medium–high, add bacon and cook, stirring, for 3 minutes. Add the flour, mustard and worcestershire sauce, and stir until combined. Cook for 1 minute. Remove from heat and gradually pour in the milk, stirring continuously until smooth. Return to the heat and stir for 5 minutes, until the mixture comes to the boil and has thickened. Stir in vegetables and the remaining stock, then add the parsley and fish. Simmer over a low heat for 5 minutes, or until heated through. Season to taste. Serve with cream.

Serves 4–6

Split pea and sweet potato soup

80 ml (2½ fl oz/⅓ cup) olive oil
1 large onion, chopped
2 garlic cloves, finely chopped
2 teaspoons finely chopped fresh
  ginger
120 g (4¼ oz/½ cup) yellow split peas
1 red chilli, seeded and sliced
½ teaspoon sweet smoked paprika
1 litre (35 fl oz/4 cups) chicken stock
500 g (1 lb 2 oz) orange sweet potato,
  cubed
1 tablespoon finely chopped mint

Heat 1 tablespoon of oil in a large saucepan over a medium heat. Fry the onion, garlic and ginger for about 5 minutes, or until soft and golden. Stir in the split peas, chilli and paprika, and cook for 1 minute. Add the stock and bring to the boil. Reduce the heat and simmer for 20 minutes.

Add sweet potato, return to the boil, then reduce the heat and simmer for 15 minutes, or until potato is tender.

Meanwhile, heat the remaining oil in a small saucepan over low heat. Stir in the mint, then immediately remove the saucepan from the heat. Transfer the mint and oil to a small dish.

Remove soup from the heat. Using an immersion blender fitted with the chopping blade, whizz for 30 seconds, or until puréed. Ladle the soup into four bowls and drizzle with a little of the minted oil.

Serves 4

Chicken and spinach orzo soup

1 tablespoon olive oil
1 leek, trimmed and cut into quarters
  lengthways, then rinsed well and
  thinly sliced
2 garlic cloves, crushed
1 teaspoon ground cumin
1.5 litres (52 fl oz/6 cups) chicken
  stock
2 boneless, skinless chicken breasts,
  about 500 g (1 lb 2 oz) in total
200 g (7 oz/1 cup) orzo (see Note)
150 g (5½ oz/3 cups) baby English
  spinach leaves, roughly chopped
1 tablespoon chopped dill
2 teaspoons lemon juice

Heat the olive oil in a large saucepan over low heat. Add the leek and sauté for 8–10 minutes, or until soft. Add garlic and cumin; cook for 1 minute.

Pour in the stock, increase the heat to high and bring to the boil. Reduce the heat to low, add the chicken breasts, then cover and simmer for 8 minutes. Remove the chicken, reserving the liquid (keep it covered over low heat to keep it hot). When the chicken is cool enough to handle, shred it finely using your fingers.

Stir the orzo into the simmering stock and simmer for 12 minutes, or until al dente.

Return the chicken to the pan and add the spinach and dill. Simmer for 2 minutes, or until the spinach has wilted. Stir in lemon juice, season to taste with sea salt and freshly ground black pepper and serve.

Serves 4

Note: Orzo is a small rice-shaped pasta, available from supermarkets.

Soups

Gazpacho

2 slices day-old white crusty bread,
  crusts removed, broken into pieces
1 kg (2 lb 4 oz) vine-ripened
  tomatoes, peeled, deseeded and
  chopped
1 red capsicum (pepper), deseeded,
  roughly chopped
2 garlic cloves, chopped
1 small green chilli, chopped (optional)
1 teaspoon caster (superfine) sugar
2 tablespoons red wine vinegar
2 tablespoons extra virgin olive oil

Garnish
1/2 Lebanese (short) cucumber,
  deseeded, finely diced
1/2 red capsicum (pepper), deseeded,
  finely diced
1/2 green capsicum (pepper),
  deseeded, finely diced
1/2 red onion, finely diced
1/2 ripe tomato, diced

Soak the bread in cold water for
5 minutes, then squeeze out any
excess liquid. Put the bread in a food
processor with the tomato, capsicum,
garlic, chilli, sugar and vinegar, and
process until combined and smooth.

With the motor running, gradually
add the oil to make a smooth creamy
mixture. Season to taste. Refrigerate
for at least 2 hours. Add a little extra
vinegar, if desired.

Combine all the ingredients for the
garnish. Spoon the chilled gazpacho
into soup bowls, top with a little
garnish and serve the remainder in
separate bowls on the side.

Serves 4

Chickpea and herb dumpling soup

1 tablespoon oil
1 onion, chopped
2 garlic cloves, crushed
2 teaspoons ground cumin
1 teaspoon ground coriander
1/4 teaspoon chilli powder
2 x 300 g (10 1/2 oz) tins chickpeas, drained
875 ml (30 fl oz/3 1/2 cups) vegetable stock
2 x 400 g (14 oz) tins chopped tomatoes
1 tablespoon chopped coriander (cilantro) leaves

Dumplings
125 g (4 1/2 oz/1 cup) self-raising flour
25 g (1 oz) butter, chopped
2 tablespoons grated parmesan cheese
2 tablespoons mixed chopped herbs (chives, flat-leaf (Italian) parsley and coriander (cilantro) leaves)
60 ml (2 fl oz/1/4 cup) full-cream (whole) milk
cracked black pepper, to serve
crusty bread, to serve

Heat the oil in a large saucepan and cook the onion over medium heat for 2–3 minutes, or until soft. Add the garlic, cumin, ground coriander and chilli, and cook for 1 minute, or until fragrant. Add the chickpeas, stock and tomato. Bring to the boil, then reduce heat and simmer, covered, for 10 minutes. Stir in coriander leaves.

To make the dumplings, sift the flour into a bowl and add the chopped butter. Rub the butter into the flour with your fingertips until it resembles fine breadcrumbs. Stir in parmesan and mixed fresh herbs. Make a well in the centre, add the milk and mix with a flat-bladed knife until just combined. Bring the dough together into a rough ball, divide into eight portions and roll into small balls.

Add dumplings to the soup, cover and simmer for about 20 minutes, or until a skewer comes out clean when inserted in the centre of the dumplings. Serve with cracked black pepper and crusty bread.

Serves 4

Lentil and silverbeet soup

Chicken stock
1 kg (2 lb 4 oz) chicken bones
  (chicken necks, backs, wings),
  washed
1 small onion, roughly chopped
1 bay leaf
3–4 flat-leaf (Italian) parsley sprigs
1–2 oregano or thyme sprigs

280 g (10 oz/1½ cups) brown lentils,
  washed
850 g (1 lb 14 oz) silverbeet
  (Swiss chard)
60 ml (2 fl oz/¼ cup) olive oil
1 large onion, finely chopped
4 garlic cloves, crushed
2 large handfuls finely chopped
  coriander (cilantro) leaves
80 ml (2½ fl oz/⅓ cup) lemon juice
lemon wedges, to serve
crusty bread, to serve

To make the stock, place all the stock ingredients in a large saucepan, add 3 litres (105 fl oz/12 cups) water and bring to the boil. Skim any scum from the surface. Reduce heat and simmer for 2 hours. Strain the stock, discarding bones, onion and herbs. Chill overnight.

Skim any fat from the stock. Place the lentils in a large saucepan and add the stock and 1 litre (35 fl oz/4 cups) water. Bring to the boil, reduce the heat and simmer, covered, for 1 hour.

Meanwhile, remove stems from the silverbeet and shred leaves. Heat the oil in a saucepan over medium heat and cook onion for 2–3 minutes, or until transparent. Add garlic and cook for 1 minute. Add the silverbeet and toss for 2–3 minutes, or until wilted. Stir mixture into the lentils. Add the coriander and lemon juice, season, and simmer, covered, for 15 minutes. Serve with the lemon wedges and crusty bread.

Serves 6

Lemon chicken soup

2 boneless, skinless chicken breasts
1 lemon
1 litre (35 fl oz/4 cups) chicken stock
2 lemon thyme sprigs, plus extra,
  to serve (see Note)

Trim excess fat from chicken. Using a vegetable peeler, cut 3 strips of zest from the lemon and remove the pith. Place the stock, 2 strips of zest and lemon thyme in a shallow saucepan and slowly bring almost to the boil. Reduce the heat to simmering point, add the chicken and cook, covered, for 7 minutes, or until the meat is cooked through. Meanwhile, cut the remaining zest into very fine strips.

Remove the chicken from the pan, transfer to a plate and cover with foil.

Strain the stock into a clean pan through a sieve lined with two layers of damp muslin (cheesecloth). Finely shred the chicken; return to the soup. Reheat gently and season to taste with salt and black pepper. Serve immediately, garnished with the extra sprigs of lemon thyme and lemon zest.

Serves 4

Note: You can use ordinary thyme if lemon thyme is not available.

Broad bean soup

350g (12 oz/2 cups) dried, skinned
   and split broad (fava) beans or
   whole dried broad (fava) beans
2 garlic cloves, peeled
1 teaspoon cumin
1 teaspoon paprika
extra virgin olive oil, cumin and
   paprika, to serve

Put broad beans in a large bowl, cover with 3 times their volume of cold water and leave to soak in a cool place for 12 hours, drain and rinse before cooking. (If using whole beans soak for 48 hours in a cool place, changing water 3–4 times. Drain; remove skins.)

Place the beans in a large soup pot, preferably stainless steel. Then add 1.25 litres (44 fl oz/5 cups) cold water, garlic and spices. Bring to the boil and simmer on low heat, covered, for 45–60 minutes, until beans are mushy; check and add a little more water if beans look dry. Do not add salt or stir the beans during cooking.

Cool slightly and then purée soup in batches in a blender, or use a stick blender and purée in the pot. Reheat soup and season to taste. Ladle into bowls and drizzle a little olive oil on each serve. Finish with a light dusting of paprika. Have extra olive oil on the table, and cumin and paprika in little bowls, to be added if desired. Serve with bread.

Serves 6

Carrot soup with caraway butter

Caraway butter
1 tablespoon caraway seeds
125 g (4½ oz) butter, softened

1 onion, chopped
1 garlic clove, crushed
750 g (1 lb 10 oz) carrots, chopped
1 litre (35 fl oz/4 cups) vegetable stock
250 ml (9 fl oz/1 cup) orange juice
rye bread, to serve

To make the butter, dry-fry the caraway seeds in a frying pan (skillet) over medium heat for 3–4 minutes, or until they start to brown and release their aroma. Leave to cool and then grind in a spice or coffee grinder until fine. Beat butter and caraway together until smooth. Place in a small square of foil, roll into a log and refrigerate for 30 minutes, or until firm.

Put the onion, garlic, carrots, stock and orange juice into a saucepan and bring to the boil. Cover and simmer over a low heat for 25 minutes, or until the carrots are cooked.

Transfer to a blender and blend until smooth. Return to the pan, season to taste and heat through. Cut the butter into 5 mm (¼ inch) thick slices.

Spoon the soup into bowls, top each with two slices of the butter and serve with some rye bread.

Serves 6

Cauliflower, cannellini bean and prosciutto soup

2 tablespoons olive oil
100 g (3½ oz/about 8 slices)
  prosciutto, chopped
1 onion, chopped
1 garlic clove, minced
800 g (1 lb 12 oz) cauliflower, cut into
  small florets
2 x 400 g (14 oz) tins cannellini beans,
  drained
125 ml (4 fl oz/½ cup) thick (double/
  heavy) cream
snipped chives, to serve

Heat 1 tablespoon of oil in a large saucepan over medium–high heat. Add prosciutto and fry, stirring often, until crisp. Transfer half the prosciutto to a plate lined with paper towels, leaving the rest in the saucepan.

Reduce heat to medium. Add the remaining oil and the onion to the pan and fry for 5 minutes, or until softened. Add the garlic and cauliflower florets and fry for 3 minutes.

Add the cannellini beans and 1 litre (35 fl oz/4 cups) of water and season well with salt and freshly ground black pepper. Bring to the boil, reduce heat and simmer, covered, for 15 minutes, or until cauliflower is tender. Set aside to cool for 10 minutes.

Using a stick blender fitted with the chopping blade, whizz the soup for 25 seconds, or until smooth. Season well with salt and freshly ground black pepper. Stir through the cream and gently reheat soup. Serve immediately, with the reserved crisp prosciutto and the chives sprinkled on top.

Serves 4

Creamy chicken and paprika soup

90 g (3¼ oz) butter
1 onion, finely chopped
1 celery stalk, finely chopped
1 small carrot, finely chopped
2 tablespoons Hungarian sweet
  paprika
40 g (1½ oz/⅓ cup) plain (all-purpose)
  flour
2 litres (70 fl oz/8 cups) chicken stock
125 ml (4 fl oz/½ cup) pouring cream
300 g (10½ oz) boneless, skinless
  cooked chicken breasts, finely
  chopped
crusty bread, to serve

In a large saucepan, melt butter over medium–high heat. Add onion, celery and carrot and cook for 5 minutes, or until the vegetables have softened.

Add paprika and cook for 1 minute, or until the paprika becomes fragrant. Quickly toss in the flour and stir until well combined. Cook for a further 1 minute and remove from heat.

Add one-third of the stock and mix to a thick paste, stirring out all the lumps. Return the pan to the heat and add remaining stock. Stir until soup boils and thickens slightly. Reduce the heat, cover and simmer for 45–50 minutes.

Remove the soup from the heat and stir in the cream and chicken. Season to taste and serve with crusty bread.

Serves 4–6

Won ton noodle soup

70 g (2½ oz) raw prawns (shrimp)
70 g (2½ oz) minced (ground) veal
3 tablespoons soy sauce
1 tablespoon finely chopped spring
  onion (scallion)
1 tablespoon finely chopped water
  chestnuts
1 teaspoon finely chopped fresh
  ginger
2 garlic cloves, finely chopped
24 gow gee wrappers
1.25 litres (44 fl oz/5 cups) chicken
  stock
2 tablespoons mirin
500 g (1 lb 2 oz) baby bok choy (pak
  choy), finely shredded
8 spring onions (scallions), sliced

Peel, devein and finely chop the prawns. Combine with minced veal, 2 teaspoons soy sauce, spring onion, water chestnuts, ginger and garlic. Lay round wrappers out on a work surface and place a teaspoon of mixture in the middle of each one.

Moisten edges of wrappers and bring up the sides to form a pouch. Pinch together to seal. Cook in batches in a large saucepan of rapidly boiling water for 4–5 minutes. Drain well and divide among soup bowls.

Bring stock, remaining soy sauce and mirin to the boil in a large saucepan. Add the bok choy, cover and simmer for 2 minutes, or until the bok choy has just wilted. Add the sliced spring onion and season. Ladle stock, bok choy and spring onion over won tons.

Serves 4

French onion soup

50 g (1¾ oz) butter
1 tablespoon olive oil
1 kg (2 lb 4 oz) onions, thinly sliced
  into rings
3 x 425 g (15 oz) tins chicken or beef
  consommé
125 ml (4 fl oz/½ cup) dry sherry
half a baguette
125g (4½ oz/1 cup) finely grated
  cheddar or gruyère cheese

Heat the butter and oil in a large saucepan, add the onion and cook, stirring frequently, over a low heat for 45 minutes, or until softened and translucent. It's important not to rush this stage — cook the onion thoroughly so that it caramelises and the flavour develops.

Add the consommé, sherry and 1 cup (9 fl oz/250 ml) water. Bring to the boil, then reduce the heat and simmer for 30 minutes. Season to taste.

Meanwhile, slice the bread into four thick slices and arrange in a single layer under a hot grill (broiler). Toast one side, remove from the grill, turn over and cover the untoasted side with the cheese.

Ladle the hot soup into four serving bowls, top each with a slice of toast, cheese side up, and place the bowls under the grill until the cheese has melted and is golden.

Serves 4

Ham and pea soup

2 tablespoons olive oil
1 large onion, chopped
3 celery stalks, sliced
about 40 sage leaves
220 g (7¾ oz/1 cup) green split peas,
  rinsed and drained
1 smoked ham hock, about 800 g
  (1 lb 12 oz)
1 thyme sprig
vegetable oil, for pan-frying

Heat the oil in a large saucepan over medium heat. Add the onion, celery and four of the sage leaves and fry, stirring often, for 5 minutes, or until the onion and celery are soft. Add the green split peas, ham hock, thyme sprig and 1.25 litres (44 fl oz/5 cups) of water. Bring to the boil, reduce the heat, cover and simmer for 1½ hours, or until the meat is falling off the bone. Remove the saucepan from the heat and discard the thyme sprig.

Remove ham hock from the saucepan and, when cool enough to handle, cut off the meat and return it to the soup. Discard the bone. With a stick blender fitted with the chopping blade, whizz the soup for 30 seconds. Season with freshly ground black pepper, and salt, if necessary.

Pour vegetable oil into a small pan to a depth of 3 cm (1¼ inches) and heat over high heat. Very carefully add the remaining sage leaves (stand back as they may spit) and fry for a few seconds, or until they turn bright green and become crisp. Remove quickly using a slotted spoon; drain on paper towels.

Gently reheat the soup and ladle into four bowls. Sprinkle fried sage leaves on top. Serve with crispbread.

Serves 4

Spicy corn and coconut soup

1 tablespoon oil
1 large onion, chopped
1 celery stalk, chopped
2 garlic cloves, chopped
1 teaspoon ground coriander
1½ teaspoons ground cumin
1–2 teaspoons sambal oelek (see Note)
500 g (1 lb 2 oz) potatoes, chopped
750 ml (26 fl oz/3 cups) chicken or vegetable stock
420 g (14¾ oz) tin corn kernels, drained
270 ml (9½ fl oz) light coconut milk
1 handful coriander (cilantro) leaves
310 g (11 oz) tin creamed corn
extra coriander (cilantro) leaves, to serve

Heat the oil in a large heavy-based saucepan over medium–low heat, then add the onion, celery and garlic. Stir for 2 minutes to coat vegetables in oil. Reduce the heat, cover and simmer, stirring occasionally, for 5 minutes. Do not allow the vegetables to brown. Add the ground coriander, cumin and 1 teaspoon of the sambal oelek and stir for 1 minute. Add potato and stock. Bring slowly to the boil, then reduce the heat and simmer, covered, for 15 minutes, or until the potato is cooked. Stir in corn kernels, coconut milk and coriander leaves. Set aside to cool slightly.

Using a stick blender fitted with the chopping blade, whizz the soup for 20–30 seconds, or until smooth. Stir in creamed corn; gently reheat soup. Add a little hot water if you prefer a thinner consistency. Season well with salt and freshly ground black pepper. Ladle into four warm bowls and add the remaining sambal oelek, to taste. Sprinkle with extra coriander leaves.

Serves 4

Note: Sambal oelek is a condiment used in Malaysian, Indonesian and Singaporean cuisines. It is made from red chillies, vinegar and sugar and is available from Asian supermarkets.

Roast pumpkin soup

1.25 kg (2 lb 12 oz) pumpkin
  (winter squash), peeled and cut
  into chunks
2 tablespoons olive oil
1 large onion, chopped
2 teaspoons ground cumin
1 large carrot, chopped
1 celery stalk, chopped
1 litre (35 fl oz/4 cups) vegetable stock
sour cream, to serve
finely chopped parsley, to serve
ground nutmeg, to serve

Preheat the oven to 180°C (350°F/ Gas 4). Put the pumpkin on a greased baking tray and lightly brush with half the olive oil. Bake for 25 minutes, or until softened and slightly browned around the edges.

Heat the remaining oil in a large saucepan. Cook the onion and cumin for 2 minutes, then add the carrot and celery and cook for 3 minutes more, stirring frequently. Add the roasted pumpkin and stock. Bring to the boil, then reduce the heat and simmer for 20 minutes.

Allow to cool a little. Purée in batches in a blender or food processor. Return the soup to the pan and gently reheat without boiling. Season to taste with salt and freshly ground black pepper. Top with sour cream and sprinkle with chopped parsley and ground nutmeg before serving.

Serves 6

Note: Butternut pumpkin is often used in soups as it has a sweeter flavour than other varieties.

Hint: If soup is too thick, thin it down with a little more stock.

Asian chicken and noodle soup

Chilli paste
4 dried chillies, roughly chopped
1 teaspoon coriander seeds
1 teaspoon grated fresh ginger
1 spring onion (scallion), chopped
½ teaspoon ground turmeric

750 ml (26 fl oz/3 cups) coconut milk
350 g (12 oz) boneless, skinless
    chicken breast, thinly sliced
2 tablespoons soy sauce
500 ml (17 fl oz/2 cups) chicken stock
400 g (14 oz) dried egg noodles
peanut oil, for deep-frying
spring onion (scallion), to serve
red chillies, to serve

To make the chilli paste, put all the ingredients in a small saucepan. Stir over low heat for 5 minutes, or until fragrant. Transfer to a mortar and pestle or food processor and grind until smooth.

Heat 250 ml (9 fl oz/1 cup) of the coconut milk in a saucepan. Add the chilli paste and stir for 2–3 minutes. Add the chicken and soy sauce and cook for 3–4 minutes. Stir in the remaining coconut milk and the stock. Bring to the boil, reduce the heat and simmer for 10 minutes.

Break a quarter of the noodles into large pieces. Fry in the hot peanut oil until crisp, then drain on paper towels. Cook the remaining noodles in boiling water until just tender, then drain.

Place the boiled noodles in serving bowls and ladle the soup over the top. Garnish with the fried noodles and serve with spring onion and chilli.

Serves 4

Leek and potato soup

50 g (1¾ oz) butter
1 onion, finely chopped
3 leeks, white part only, sliced
1 celery stalk, finely chopped
1 garlic clove, finely chopped
200 g (7 oz) potatoes, chopped
750 ml (27 fl oz/3 cups) chicken stock
220 ml (7½ fl oz) pouring cream
2 tablespoons chopped chives

Melt the butter in a large saucepan. Add the onion, leek, celery and garlic. Cover pan and cook, stirring occasionally, over a low heat for 15 minutes, or until vegetables are softened but not browned. Add potato and stock and bring to the boil.

Reduce the heat and leave to simmer, covered, for 20 minutes. Allow soup to cool a little before puréeing in a blender or food processor, then return to the cleaned saucepan.

Bring the soup gently back to the boil and stir in the cream. Season with salt and white pepper and reheat without boiling. Serve either hot or well chilled. Garnish with chives.

Serves 6

Spiced lentil soup

1 eggplant (aubergine)
60 ml (2 fl oz/¼ cup) olive oil
1 onion, finely chopped
2 teaspoons brown mustard seeds
2 teaspoons ground cumin
1 teaspoon garam masala
¼ teaspoon cayenne pepper (optional)
2 large carrots, cut into cubes
1 celery stalk, diced
400 g (14 oz) tin chopped tomatoes
100 g (3½ oz/1 cup) puy or small
   blue-green lentils
1 litre (35 fl oz/4 cups) chicken stock
2 large handfuls coriander (cilantro)
   leaves, roughly chopped
125 g (4½ oz/½ cup) plain yoghurt

Cut the eggplant into cubes, place in a colander, sprinkle with salt and leave for 20 minutes. Rinse well and pat the eggplant dry with paper towels.

Heat the oil in a large saucepan over medium heat. Add the onion and cook for 5 minutes, or until softened. Add eggplant, stir to coat in oil and cook for 3 minutes, or until softened.

Add the spices and the cayenne pepper (if using) and cook, stirring, for 1 minute, or until fragrant and the mustard seeds begin to pop. Add carrot and celery; cook for 1 minute. Stir in the tomato, lentils and stock and bring to the boil. Reduce heat and simmer for 40 minutes, or until the lentils are tender and the liquid is reduced to a thick stew-like soup. Season to taste with salt and freshly ground black pepper.

Stir the coriander into the soup just before serving. Ladle the soup into four warmed bowls and serve with a dollop of the yoghurt on top.

Serves 4

Portuguese chicken broth with rice

2.5 litres (87 fl oz/10 cups) chicken stock
1 onion, cut into thin wedges
1 teaspoon grated lemon zest
1 mint sprig
500 g (1 lb 2 oz) potatoes, chopped
1 tablespoon olive oil
2 boneless, skinless chicken breasts
200 g (7 oz/1 cup) long-grain rice
2 tablespoons lemon juice
mint leaves, to garnish

Combine the chicken stock, onion, lemon zest, mint sprig, potato and olive oil in a large saucepan. Slowly bring to the boil, then reduce the heat, add the chicken breasts and simmer gently for 20–25 minutes, or until the chicken is cooked through.

Remove the chicken breasts and discard the mint sprig. Cool the chicken, then cut it into thin slices.

Meanwhile, add rice to the saucepan and simmer for 25–30 minutes, or until rice is tender. Return the sliced chicken to the saucepan, add lemon juice and stir for 1–2 minutes, or until the chicken is warmed through. Season and serve garnished with the mint leaves.

Serves 6

Note: Rice and potato absorb liquid on standing, so serve immediately.

Zucchini and basil soup

1 large onion, finely chopped
3 garlic cloves, very finely chopped
1/2 teaspoon coriander seeds
2 celery stalks, finely diced
6 zucchini (courgettes), roughly diced
3 large waxy potatoes, diced
1.25 litres (44 fl oz/5 cups) chicken
   stock
125 g (4 1/2 oz/1/2 cup) crème fraîche
   or sour cream
1 large handful basil, torn
2 tablespoons finely chopped flat-leaf
   (Italian) parsley
sea salt, to serve

Place onion, garlic, coriander seeds, celery, zucchini, potato and stock in a large heavy-based saucepan. Bring to the boil over medium heat. Partially cover the pan and gently simmer for 12–15 minutes, or until all vegetables are cooked through.

Meanwhile, put the crème fraîche or sour cream in a small bowl with half the basil and the parsley. Combine, using a fork, then set aside.

Remove the saucepan from the heat. Using an immersion blender fitted with the chopping blade, whizz the soup for 20 seconds, or until semi-smooth. Stir in the remaining basil. Season with salt and freshly ground black pepper, to taste.

Divide crème fraîche mixture among four bowls and ladle in the soup. Sprinkle with sea salt and freshly ground black pepper and serve.

Serves 4

Potato, broccoli and cauliflower soup

500 g (1 lb 2 oz) broccoli
cooking oil spray
2 onions, finely chopped
2 garlic cloves, finely chopped
2 teaspoons ground cumin
1 teaspoon ground coriander
750 g (1 lb 10 oz) potatoes, cubed
2 small chicken stock (bouillon) cubes
375 ml (13 fl oz/1½ cups) skim milk
3 tablespoons finely chopped
    coriander (cilantro)

Cut the broccoli into small pieces. Lightly spray base of a large saucepan with oil and place over medium heat. Add the onion and garlic and 1 tablespoon water. Cover the pan. Cook, stirring occasionally, over low heat for 5 minutes, or until the onion has softened and is lightly golden. Add the ground cumin and coriander and cook for 2 minutes.

Add the potato and broccoli to the pan, stir well and add the stock cubes and 1 litre (35 fl oz/4 cups) water. Slowly bring to the boil, reduce the heat, cover and simmer over low heat for 20 minutes, or until the vegetables are tender. Allow to cool slightly.

Blend the soup in batches in a food processor or blender until smooth. Return to the pan and stir in the milk. Slowly reheat, without boiling. Stir the chopped coriander through and season well before serving.

Serves 6

Pasta,
Noodles
& Rice

Rigatoni with sausage, fennel seed and tomato

2 garlic cloves, chopped
2 teaspoons fennel seeds
3 tablespoons olive oil
1 onion, finely chopped
4 Italian sausages, skin removed
1 tablespoon chopped thyme leaves
100 ml (3½ fl oz) red wine
400 g (14 oz) tinned chopped
   tomatoes
400 g (14 oz) rigatoni
grated parmesan cheese, to serve

Using a mortar and pestle, crush the garlic and fennel seeds with a pinch of salt. Alternatively, grind the seeds in a spice grinder and crush the garlic.

Heat the oil in a saucepan and cook onion for a few minutes over low heat to soften it. Break up the sausage meat with your hands and add it to the pan. Increase the heat and cook until the meat is lightly browned. Season with salt and pepper. Add the garlic, fennel and thyme, mix briefly, then add the wine. Stir the sauce, scraping up any sausage meat that may be stuck to the bottom of the pan—this will add flavour to the sauce.

Cook sauce for about 5 minutes or until the wine is reduced, then add the tomatoes and simmer for 10 minutes or until the sauce has thickened.

Cook pasta in a large saucepan of boiling salted water until al dente. Drain pasta briefly, leaving some water clinging to the pasta. Add to sauce, toss well and serve with parmesan.

Serves 4

Spaghetti with rocket and chilli

500 g (1 lb 2 oz) spaghetti or
  spaghettini
2 tablespoons olive oil
2 teaspoons finely chopped small
  red chilli
450 g (1 lb) rocket (arugula) leaves
1 tablespoon lemon juice
shaved parmesan cheese, to serve

Cook the pasta in a large saucepan of rapidly boiling salted water until al dente. Drain and return to the pan.

Meanwhile, heat the olive oil in a large frying pan. Add the chilli and cook for 1 minute over low heat. Add the rocket and cook, stirring often, for a further 2–3 minutes, or until softened. Add lemon juice and season with sea salt and freshly ground black pepper.

Add rocket mixture to the pasta and toss to combine well. Serve scattered with shaved parmesan.

Serves 4–6

Chinese fried rice

2 tablespoons peanut oil
2 eggs, lightly beaten and seasoned
2 teaspoons lard (optional)
1 onion, cut into wedges
250 g (9 oz) ham, cut into thin strips
750 g (1 lb 10 oz/4 cups) cold cooked
   rice (see Note)
3 tablespoons frozen peas
2 tablespoons soy sauce
4 spring onions (scallions), cut into
   short lengths
250 g (9 oz) cooked small prawns
   (shrimp), peeled

Heat 1 tablespoon peanut oil in a wok or large frying pan and add the eggs, pulling the set egg towards the centre and tilting the wok to let the unset egg run to the edge.

When it is almost set, break up the egg into large pieces to resemble scrambled eggs. Transfer to a plate.

Heat the remaining oil and lard in the wok, swirling to coat base and side. Add the onion and stir-fry over high heat until clear and softened. Add the ham and stir-fry for 1 minute. Add the rice and peas and stir-fry for 3 minutes until the rice is heated through. Add the eggs, soy sauce, spring onion and prawns. Heat through and serve.

Serves 4

Note: Rice should be refrigerated overnight before making fried rice to let the grains dry out and separate.

Variation: This dish is traditionally served as a snack or a course in its own right rather than as an accompaniment. You can include Chinese barbecued pork (char siu), Chinese sausage (lap cheong) or bacon instead of ham.

Macaroni cheese

225 g (8 oz) macaroni
80 g (2¾ oz) butter
1 onion, finely chopped
3 tablespoons plain (all-purpose) flour
500 ml (17 fl oz/2 cups) milk
2 teaspoons wholegrain mustard
250 g (9 oz) cheddar cheese, grated
30 g (1 oz) fresh breadcrumbs

Cook the pasta in rapidly boiling salted water until al dente. Drain. Preheat the oven to 180°C (350°F/Gas 4) and grease a casserole dish.

Melt the butter in a large saucepan over low heat and cook onion for 5 minutes, or until softened. Stir in the flour and cook for 1 minute, or until pale and foaming. Remove from the heat and gradually stir in the milk. Return to the heat and stir until the sauce boils and thickens. Reduce the heat and simmer for 2 minutes. Stir in the mustard and about three-quarters of the cheese. Season to taste.

Mix the pasta with the cheese sauce. Spoon into the dish and sprinkle the breadcrumbs and remaining cheese over the top. Bake for 15 minutes, or until golden brown and bubbling.

Serves 4

Chicken and noodles with honey lime dressing

Dressing
3 tablespoons honey
4 tablespoons light soy sauce
zest and juice from 2 limes
2 Asian shallots, finely chopped
1 teaspoon grated fresh ginger
1 small red chilli, seeded and finely
  chopped

1 lb 2 oz (500 g) Singapore noodles
1 barbecued chicken, skin and fat
  removed
150 g (5½ oz/1½ cups) snowpeas
  (mangetout), trimmed and cut in
  half on the diagonal
180 g (6½ oz/2 cups) bean sprouts
2 celery stalks, cut into thin, 5 cm
  (2 inch) long shreds
2 large handfuls mint

Combine dressing ingredients in a small bowl. Place the noodles in a bowl, pour over boiling water and leave for 1 minute to soften. Drain. Refresh under cold water, then cut into short lengths using scissors. Place in a large mixing bowl.

Shred the flesh from the chicken. Blanch the snowpeas in a saucepan of boiling water. Boil for 1 minute, then drain and refresh. Add the snowpeas to the noodles. Add the chicken meat to the noodles.

Add the bean sprouts, celery, mint leaves and dressing and toss well to combine. Serve immediately.

Serves 4

Hints: You can use any thin noodles. Cook according to the manufacturer's directions.

If you want to reduce the fat in this meal, use freshly cooked chicken meat instead of barbecued chicken.

Penne with spring vegetables and pesto

Basil pesto
225 g (8 oz/2 bunches) basil
80 g (2¾ oz/½ cup) pine nuts
1 garlic clove, roughly chopped
30 g (1 oz/⅓ cup) grated pecorino
  cheese, plus extra, to serve
1 red chilli, roughly chopped
185 ml (6 fl oz/¾ cup) olive oil

200 g (7 oz) broccoli, chopped into
  florets
100 g (3½ oz) button mushrooms,
  sliced
1 carrot, cut into thin strips
175 g (6 oz/1 bunch) asparagus,
  trimmed and cut into 2 cm (¾ inch)
  lengths
500 g (1 lb 2 oz) penne
½ red capsicum (pepper), cut into
  thin strips

To make the pesto, put the basil, pine nuts, garlic, pecorino and chilli in a food processor and blend until finely chopped. With motor running, add the olive oil in a thin stream and process until well combined. Season to taste.

Line a large steamer with baking paper and punch with holes. Arrange the broccoli, mushrooms, carrot and asparagus in a single layer on top and cover with a lid. Sit the steamer over a saucepan or wok of simmering water and steam for about 4–5 minutes, or until just cooked.

Meanwhile, cook the penne in a large saucepan of rapidly boiling salted water for 10 minutes, or until al dente. Drain well and return to the pan. Add steamed vegetables, capsicum and pesto and mix well. Serve hot or cold with extra pecorino.

Serves 4

Ham and cheese pasta bake

1½ tablespoons olive oil
1 onion, finely chopped
300 g (10½ oz) leg ham, sliced 3 mm
  (⅛ inch) thick and cut into 5 cm
  (2 inch) lengths
600 ml (21 fl oz) pouring cream
300 g (10½ oz) cooked fresh peas
  or frozen peas, thawed
375 g (13 oz) conchiglione
3 tablespoons roughly chopped basil
250 g (9 oz) grated mature cheddar
  cheese

Preheat oven to 200°C (400°F/Gas 6). Lightly grease a 2.5 litre (87 fl oz/ 10 cup) ovenproof ceramic dish.

Heat 1 tablespoon of oil in a frying pan over medium heat. Cook onion, stirring, for 5 minutes or until soft. Add the remaining oil, then the ham and cook, stirring, for 1 minute. Add cream and bring to the boil. Reduce heat and simmer for 6 minutes. Add the peas and cook for 3 minutes, or until mixture has thickened slightly. Season well.

Meanwhile, cook the pasta in a large saucepan of boiling salted water until al dente. Drain well and return to the pan to keep warm.

Add sauce to the pasta, then stir in basil and three-quarters of the cheese. Season. Add mixture to the prepared dish, sprinkle on the remaining cheese and bake for 20 minutes, or until the top is golden brown.

Serves 4

Red wine risotto

500 ml (17 fl oz/2 cups) chicken stock
1 thyme sprig
100 g (3½ oz) butter
1 onion, finely chopped
1 large garlic clove, finely chopped
225 g (8 oz) risotto rice
500 ml (17 fl oz/2 cups) dry red wine
25 g (1 oz) parmesan cheese, grated,
  plus extra to serve

Heat the chicken stock in a saucepan and maintain at a low simmer.

Strip the leaves from the thyme sprig.

Melt the butter in a deep heavy-based frying pan and gently cook the onion and garlic until soft but not browned. Add the thyme and rice and reduce the heat to low. Season and stir to coat the grains of rice in the butter.

Add half the red wine to the rice and increase the heat to medium. Cook, stirring, until all the liquid is absorbed. Stir in half the stock and cook at a fast simmer, stirring constantly. When the stock has been absorbed, stir in the rest of the wine.

Stir in nearly all the remaining stock and cook until the rice is al dente. Add a little more stock or water if you need to; every risotto is different.

Stir in the parmesan and sprinkle a little extra over the top to serve.

Serves 4

Spaghetti Bolognese

60 g (2¼ oz) butter
1 onion, finely chopped
2 garlic cloves, crushed
1 celery stalk, finely chopped
1 carrot, diced
50 g (1¾ oz) pancetta, diced
500 g (1 lb 2 oz) minced (ground) beef
1 tablespoon chopped oregano
250 ml (9 fl oz/1 cup) dry red wine
500 ml (17 fl oz/2 cups) beef stock
2 tablespoons tomato paste
   (concentrated purée)
800 g (1 lb 12 oz) tinned crushed
   tomatoes
400 g (14 oz) spaghetti
3 tablespoons grated parmesan
   cheese, to serve

Melt the butter in a large saucepan over medium heat. Add the onion and cook for 2–3 minutes, or until soft. Add garlic, celery and carrot, and cook, stirring, over low heat, for 5 minutes. Increase the heat to high, add pancetta, beef and oregano, and cook for 5 minutes, or until browned.

Pour in the wine, reduce the heat and simmer for 4–5 minutes, or until absorbed. Add ccstock, tomato paste and tomatoes, and season. Cover with a lid and simmer for 1½ hours, stirring occasionally. Uncover and simmer for a further 1 hour, stirring occasionally.

Cook the pasta in a large saucepan of boiling salted water until al dente. Drain well and return to the pan to keep warm. Top the pasta with the sauce. Serve with the parmesan.

Serves 4

Capsicum, snowpea and hokkien noodle stir-fry

500 g (1 lb 2 oz) hokkien (egg)
  noodles
1 tablespoon vegetable or peanut oil
1 red onion, cut into thin wedges
2 garlic cloves, crushed
3 cm (1¼ inch) piece fresh ginger,
  thinly sliced
150 g (5½ oz) snowpeas (mangetout),
  topped and tailed, large ones halved
  on the diagonal
1 carrot, halved lengthways, sliced on
  the diagonal
1 red capsicum (pepper), thinly sliced
4 tablespoons Chinese barbecue
  sauce (char siu sauce)
1 handful coriander (cilantro) leaves

Soak the noodles in boiling water for
5 minutes to soften and separate;
drain well.

Heat a wok over high heat, add oil
and swirl to coat. Add onion, garlic
and ginger and stir-fry for 1 minute.
Add snowpeas, carrot and capsicum
and cook for 2–3 minutes. Stir in the
noodles and barbecue sauce; cook
for a further 2 minutes. Toss in the
coriander leaves and serve.

Serves 4 as a side dish

Farfalle with spinach and bacon

400 g (14 oz) farfalle
2 tablespoons extra virgin olive oil
250 g (9 oz) bacon, chopped
1 red onion, finely chopped
250 g (9 oz) baby English spinach
  leaves, stalks trimmed
1–2 tablespoons sweet chilli sauce
  (optional)
35 g (1 1/4 oz/1/4 cup) crumbled goat's
  cheese

Cook the pasta in a large saucepan of boiling salted water until al dente. Drain well and return to the pan to keep warm.

Meanwhile, heat the oil in a frying pan over medium heat. Add the bacon and cook for 3 minutes, or until golden. Add the onion and cook for a further 4 minutes, or until softened. Toss the spinach leaves through the onion and bacon mixture for 30 seconds, or until just wilted.

Add the bacon and spinach mixture to the pasta, then stir in the sweet chilli sauce, if using. Season and toss well. Scatter with the crumbled goat's cheese to serve.

Serves 4

Roasted vegetable cannelloni

60 g (2¼ oz) butter
1 large leek, cut into 1 cm (½ inch) pieces
200 g (7 oz) chargrilled eggplant (aubergine) in oil
200 g (7 oz) chargrilled orange sweet potato in oil
125 g (4½ oz/1 cup) grated cheddar cheese
40 g (1½ oz/⅓ cup) plain (all-purpose) flour
1 litre (35 fl oz/4 cups) milk
6 fresh lasagne sheets

Preheat the oven to 200°C (400°F/ Gas 6). Lightly grease a 28 x 18 x 5 cm (11¼ x 7 x 2 inch) ceramic dish. Melt 20 g (¾ oz) of the butter in a saucepan, add the leek and stir over medium heat for 8 minutes, or until soft. Chop the eggplant and sweet potato into 1 cm (½ inch) pieces and place in a bowl. Mix in the leek and 40 g (1½ oz/⅓ cup) of the cheddar.

Melt remaining butter in a saucepan over medium heat. Stir in the flour and cook for 1 minute, or until foaming. Remove from the heat and gradually stir in the milk. Return to the heat and stir until the sauce boils and thickens. Reduce heat and simmer for 2 minutes. Season. Stir 375 ml (13 fl oz/1½ cups) of sauce into the vegetable mixture, adding extra, if necessary, to bind it together.

Cut lasagne sheets in half widthways to make two smaller rectangles. Spoon the vegetable mixture along the centre of one sheet and roll up. Repeat to make 12 tubes. Place the tubes in the dish, seam-side down and spoon the remaining sauce over the top. Sprinkle with the remaining cheese and bake for 20 minutes, or until the top is golden.

Serves 4

Pork and caraway pilaf

2 tablespoons oil
400 g (14 oz) diced lean pork
1 large onion, diced
2 garlic cloves, crushed
1 tablespoon caraway seeds
300 g (10½ oz/1½ cups) basmati rice,
   rinsed until water runs clear
750 ml (26 fl oz/3 cups) chicken stock
125 g (4½ oz/½ cup) plain yoghurt
2 tablespoons chopped coriander
   (cilantro) leaves

Heat oil in a large frying pan over medium–high heat. Cook pork until brown, then remove from the pan.

Add the onion and garlic to the pan and cook for 3–5 minutes, or until the onion has softened. Add caraway seeds and rice. Cook for 2 minutes, stirring frequently, or until the rice is glossy and spices fragrant.

Add pork, pour in the stock and bring to the boil. Reduce heat to a simmer. Cover and cook for 15–20 minutes, or until the rice and pork is cooked.

Season to taste and serve topped with a dollop of yoghurt and the coriander.

Serves 4

Spaghettini with anchovies, capers and chilli

400 g (14 oz) spaghettini
125 ml (4 fl oz/½ cup) olive oil
4 garlic cloves, finely chopped
10 anchovy fillets, chopped
1 tablespoon baby capers, rinsed and
  squeezed dry
1 teaspoon chilli flakes
2 tablespoons lemon juice
2 teaspoons finely grated lemon zest
3 tablespoons chopped flat-leaf
  (Italian) parsley
3 tablespoons chopped basil leaves
3 tablespoons chopped mint
50 g (1¾ oz/½ cup) coarsely grated
  parmesan cheese, plus extra,
  to serve
extra virgin olive oil, to drizzle

Cook the pasta in a large saucepan of boiling salted water until al dente. Drain well and return to the pan to keep warm.

Heat oil in a frying pan over medium heat. Cook the garlic for 2–3 minutes, or until starting to brown. Add the anchovies, capers and chilli and cook for 1 minute.

Add pasta to the pan with the lemon juice, zest, parsley, basil, mint and parmesan. Season and toss together.

To serve, drizzle with a little extra oil and sprinkle with the parmesan.

Serves 4

Chilli and tofu stir-fry

3 tablespoons peanut oil
1 teaspoon bottled crushed chilli
2 teaspoons grated fresh ginger
2 garlic cloves, crushed
250 g (9 oz) hard tofu, cut into 1.5 cm
   (5/8 inch) cubes
8 spring onions (scallions), sliced on
   the diagonal
150 g (5½ oz) fresh baby corn, halved
   lengthways
150 g (5½ oz) snowpeas (mangetout),
   topped and tailed
500 (1 lb 2 oz) hokkien (egg) noodles
40 g (1½ oz/¼ cup) cashew nuts
2 tablespoons soy sauce
125 ml (4 fl oz/½ cup) vegetable stock
1 handful coriander (cilantro) leaves

Heat oil in a wok over medium heat
and swirl to coat. Add chilli, ginger
and garlic and stir-fry 2–3 minutes,
or until aromatic. Add the tofu cubes,
spring onion and baby corn and stir-
fry for 2–3 minutes.

Add snowpeas, noodles and cashews
and cook, stirring, for 3 minutes, or
until the vegetables are almost tender.
Stir in soy sauce and stock, bring to
the boil and simmer for 2 minutes, or
until liquid is slightly reduced. Stir in
the coriander and serve immediately.

Serves 6

Pasta with fresh chilli and herbs

500 g (1 lb 2 oz) pasta, such as
  fettucine
125 ml (4 fl oz/½ cup) olive oil
5 garlic cloves, very finely chopped
3–4 small red chillies, deseeded and
  very finely sliced
4 anchovies, very finely chopped
1 large handful flat-leaf (Italian)
  parsley, roughly chopped
1 small handful oregano, finely
  chopped
1 small handful basil, chopped
2 tablespoons lemon juice
shaved parmesan cheese, to serve

Bring a large saucepan of salted water
to the boil. Cook the pasta according
to packet instructions until al dente,
then drain.

Meanwhile, place olive oil, garlic, chilli
and anchovies in a small saucepan
over low heat and cook, stirring, for
10 minutes, or until the garlic is lightly
golden. Remove from the heat.

Add oil mixture to the drained pasta
with the parsley, oregano, basil and
lemon juice. Toss to combine. Season
to taste. Serve with shaved parmesan.

Serves 4

Minced pork and noodle salad

1 tablespoon peanut oil
500 g (1 lb 2 oz) minced (ground) pork
2 garlic cloves, finely chopped
1 lemon grass stem, finely chopped
2–3 red Asian shallots, thinly sliced
3 teaspoons finely grated ginger
1 small red chilli, finely chopped
5 makrut (kaffir lime) leaves, very finely
   shredded
170 g (6 oz) glass (mung bean)
   noodles
60 g (2 oz) baby English spinach
   leaves
60 g (2 oz) roughly chopped coriander
   (cilantro)
170 g (6 oz) peeled, finely chopped
   fresh pineapple
1 large handful mint leaves

Dressing
1½ tablespoons shaved palm sugar
   (jaggery) or soft brown sugar
6 tablespoons fish sauce
4 tablespoons lime juice
2 teaspoons sesame oil
2 teaspoons peanut oil, extra

Heat a wok until very hot, add the peanut oil and swirl to coat the wok. Add the pork and stir-fry in batches over high heat for 5 minutes, or until lightly golden. Add the garlic, lemon grass, shallots, grated ginger, chilli and lime leaves, and stir-fry for a further 1–2 minutes, or until fragrant.

Place noodles in a large bowl and cover with boiling water for about 30 seconds, or until softened. Rinse under cold water and drain well. Toss in a bowl with the spinach, coriander, pineapple, mint and pork mixture.

To make the dressing, mix together the palm sugar, fish sauce and lime juice. Add the sesame oil and extra peanut oil, and whisk to combine. Toss through the salad and season with freshly ground black pepper.

Serves 4

Spaghetti alla puttanesca

1 small red chilli
1 tablespoon capers
4 tablespoons olive oil
1 small onion, finely chopped
2 garlic cloves, finely sliced
6 anchovy fillets, finely chopped
400 g (14 oz) tinned chopped
   tomatoes
1 tablespoon finely chopped oregano
   or ¼ teaspoon dried oregano
100 g (3½ oz) black olives, pitted
   and halved
400 g (14 oz) spaghetti
1 tablespoon finely chopped parsley

Cut the chilli in half, remove the seeds and then chop chilli finely. Rinse the capers, squeeze them dry and, if they are large, chop them roughly.

Heat olive oil in a large saucepan and add onion, garlic and chilli. Fry gently for about 6 minutes, or until the onion is soft. Add the anchovies and cook, stirring and mashing, until they break down to a smooth paste.

Add the tomatoes, oregano, olives and capers and bring to the boil. Reduce the heat, season and leave to simmer for about 10 minutes, or until the sauce has reduced and thickened.

Meanwhile, cook the pasta in a large saucepan of boiling salted water until al dente. Drain briefly, leaving some of the water still clinging to the pasta, then add to the sauce with the parsley. Toss well before serving.

Serves 4

Shish kebabs with risoni salad

Risoni salad
200 g (7 oz/1 cup) risoni
2 teaspoons extra virgin olive oil
2 teaspoons balsamic vinegar
1/2 teaspoon grated lemon zest
2 teaspoons lemon juice
40 g (1 3/4 oz) baby rocket (arugula)
  leaves
1 1/2 tablespoons shredded basil leaves
1/2 small red onion, finely sliced

Shish kebabs
250 g (9 oz) minced (ground) lamb
250 g (9 oz) minced (ground) veal
1 onion, finely chopped
2 garlic cloves, crushed
1 teaspoon ground allspice
1 teaspoon ground cinnamon
oil, for brushing

To make the risoni salad, bring a saucepan of salted water to the boil, add risoni and cook for 12 minutes, or until tender. Drain, rinse under cold water, then drain again. Put the risoni in a large bowl with the oil, vinegar, lemon zest, lemon juice, rocket, basil and onion. Mix well, season to taste with salt and pepper and refrigerate until ready to serve.

To make the shish kebabs, put the lamb, veal, onion, garlic, allspice and cinnamon in a food processor with a little salt and pepper. Blend until fine, but not mushy. Divide the mixture into eight equal portions, then roll into long sausage-shaped shish kebabs. Insert a long metal skewer through the middle of each shish kebab, pressing the mixture firmly onto the skewers. Refrigerate for 30 minutes to firm.

Preheat a barbecue grill plate, flat plate or chargrill pan to medium. Brush the hotplate with oil and grill the kebabs for about 8–10 minutes, or until cooked through, turning often. Serve warm with the risoni salad.

Serves 4

Sesame tofu rice

300 g (10½ oz) firm tofu
2 teaspoons sesame oil
2 tablespoons soy sauce
1 tablespoon sesame seeds
2 tablespoons oil
3 zucchini (courgettes), sliced
150 g (5½ oz) button mushrooms,
  halved or quartered
1 large red capsicum (pepper),
  cut into squares
2 garlic cloves, crushed
550 g (1 lb 4 oz/3 cups) cold cooked
  brown rice (see Note)
1–2 tablespoons soy sauce, extra

Drain the tofu and pat dry with paper towels. Cut into cubes, place in a glass or ceramic bowl and add the sesame oil and soy sauce. Stir well and put in the refrigerator to marinate for 30 minutes, stirring occasionally.

Heat the wok until very hot, add the sesame seeds and dry-fry until lightly golden. Tip onto a plate to cool.

Reheat the wok, add oil and swirl it around to coat the side. Remove tofu from bowl with a slotted spoon and reserve the marinade. Stir-fry the tofu over high heat, turning occasionally, for about 3 minutes, or until browned. Remove from the wok and set aside.

Add the vegetables and garlic, and cook, stirring often, until they are just tender. Add rice and tofu, and stir-fry until heated through.

Add the toasted sesame seeds, the reserved marinade and the extra soy sauce to taste. Toss to coat the tofu and vegetables. Serve immediately.

Serves 4

Note: Rice should be refrigerated overnight before making fried rice to let the grains dry out and separate.

Spaghetti with meatballs

Meatballs
500 g (1 lb 2 oz) minced (ground) beef
40 g (1½ oz) fresh breadcrumbs
1 onion, finely chopped
2 garlic cloves, crushed
2 teaspoons worcestershire sauce
1 teaspoon dried oregano
30 g (1 oz/¼ cup) plain (all-purpose)
   flour
2 tablespoons olive oil

Sauce
800 g (1 lb 12 oz) tinned chopped
   tomatoes
1 tablespoon olive oil
1 onion, finely chopped
2 garlic cloves, crushed
2 tablespoons tomato paste
   (concentrated purée)
120 ml (4 fl oz) beef stock
2 teaspoons sugar

500 g (1 lb 2 oz) spaghetti
grated parmesan cheese, to serve

Combine the beef, breadcrumbs, onion, garlic, worcestershire sauce and oregano in a bowl and season. Mix well. Roll level tablespoons of the mixture into balls, dust with the flour and shake off the excess. Heat oil in a frying pan over high heat. Cook the meatballs in batches, turning, until browned all over. Drain well.

Purée tomatoes in a food processor. Heat oil in a frying pan over medium heat. Add onion and cook until soft. Add garlic and cook for 1 minute. Add puréed tomatoes, tomato paste, stock and sugar and stir to combine. Bring to the boil, add the meatballs, reduce the heat and simmer for 15 minutes. Season well.

Meanwhile, cook the pasta in a large saucepan of boiling salted water until al dente. Drain well and return to the pan to keep warm.

Top the pasta with the meatballs and sauce. Serve with parmesan.

Serves 4

Vegetarian pad thai

400 g (14 oz) flat rice-stick noodles
2 tablespoons peanut oil
2 eggs, lightly beaten
1 onion, cut into thin wedges
2 garlic cloves, crushed
1 small red capsicum (pepper), thinly
   sliced
100 g (3½ oz) fried tofu, cut into thin
   strips
6 spring onions (scallions), thinly sliced
2 very large handfuls coriander
   (cilantro) leaves, chopped
60 ml (2 fl oz/¼ cup) soy sauce
2 tablespoons lime juice
1 tablespoon soft brown sugar
2 teaspoons sambal oelek
90 g (3¼ oz/1 cup) bean sprouts
3 tablespoons chopped roasted
   unsalted peanuts

Cook the noodles in a saucepan of boiling water for 5–10 minutes, or until tender. Drain and set aside.

Heat a wok over high heat and add enough peanut oil to coat the bottom and side. When smoking, add the egg and swirl to form a thin omelette. Cook for 30 seconds, or until just set. Roll up, remove and thinly slice.

Heat remaining oil in the wok. Add the onion, garlic and capsicum, and cook over high heat for 2–3 minutes, or until the onion softens. Add the noodles, tossing well. Stir in the omelette, tofu, spring onion and half the coriander.

Pour in the combined soy sauce, lime juice, sugar and sambal oelek, then toss to coat the noodles. Sprinkle with the bean sprouts and top with roasted peanuts and the remaining coriander. Serve immediately.

Serves 4

Fettucine with zucchini

500 g (1 lb 2 oz) fettucine or tagliatelle
60 g (2¼ oz) butter
2 garlic cloves, crushed
500 g (1 lb 2 oz) zucchini (courgettes),
  grated
75 g (2½ oz/¾ cup) grated parmesan
  cheese
250 ml (9 fl oz/1 cup) olive oil
16 basil leaves (see Hint)

Cook the pasta in a large saucepan of rapidly boiling salted water until al dente. Drain well and return to the pan to keep warm.

Meanwhile, heat the butter in a deep heavy-based saucepan over low heat until it is foaming. Add garlic and cook for 1 minute. Add zucchini and cook, stirring occasionally, for 1–2 minutes or until zucchini has softened.

Add the sauce to the pasta. Add the parmesan and toss well.

To make basil leaves crisp, heat the oil in a small saucepan, add two leaves at a time and cook for 1 minute or until crisp. Drain on paper towels. Serve with the pasta.

Serves 4–6

Hint: Basil leaves can be fried up to 2 hours in advance of preparing this dish. Store in an airtight container after cooling.

Spiced basmati and nut rice

small pinch saffron threads
250 g (9 oz/1¼ cups) basmati rice
2 tablespoons vegetable oil
2 cinnamon sticks
6 green cardamom pods, crushed
6 cloves
75 g (2½ oz/½ cup) blanched
　almonds, toasted
75 g (2½ oz/scant ⅔ cup) raisins
1 teaspoon salt
2 tablespoons chopped coriander
　(cilantro) leaves

Soak saffron threads in 3 tablespoons of boiling water until required. Put the rice in a sieve and wash under cold running water until water runs clear.

Heat the oil in a saucepan, add the spices and fry gently over medium heat for 1–2 minutes, or until they start to release their aroma. Add the rice, nuts and raisins and stir well until all the grains are glossy. Add 500 ml (17 fl oz/2 cups) of cold water and the salt, and bring to the boil. Cover and simmer gently over a low heat for 15 minutes.

Remove pan from the heat, remove the lid, and drizzle over the saffron water. Cover and leave to stand for a further 10 minutes. Stir through the coriander and serve.

Serves 4

Somen noodle salad with sesame dressing

Sesame dressing
4 tablespoons sesame seeds, toasted
2½ tablespoons light soy sauce
2 tablespoons rice vinegar
2 teaspoons sugar
½ teaspoon grated ginger
½ teaspoon dashi granules

125 g (4½ oz) dried somen noodles
100 g (3½ oz) snowpeas (mangetout),
  finely sliced on the diagonal
100 g (3½ oz) daikon radish, thinly
  sliced
1 small carrot, cut into very thin slices
1 spring onion (scallion), sliced on the
  diagonal
50 g (2 oz) baby English spinach
  leaves, trimmed
2 teaspoons sesame seeds, toasted

To make the dressing, place sesame seeds in a mortar and pestle and grind until fine and moist. Combine soy sauce, rice vinegar, sugar, ginger, dashi granules and 125 ml (4 fl oz/ ½ cup) water in a small saucepan and bring to the boil over high heat. Reduce heat to medium and simmer, stirring, for 2 minutes, or until dashi granules have dissolved. Remove from heat. Cool. Gradually combine with the ground sesame seeds, stirring to form a thick dressing.

Cook the noodles in a large saucepan of boiling water for 2 minutes, or until tender. Drain, rinse under cold water and cool completely. Cut into 10 cm (4 inch) lengths using scissors.

Place the snowpeas in a large shallow bowl with the daikon, carrot, spring onion, English spinach leaves and the noodles. Add dressing and toss well to combine. Place in the refrigerator until ready to serve. When serving, sprinkle with toasted sesame seeds.

Serves 4

Penne with zucchini, ricotta and parmesan sauce

500 g (1 lb 2 oz/5½ cups) small
  penne pasta

Sauce
2 zucchini (courgettes), chopped
2 garlic cloves, chopped
1 small red chilli, deseeded and
  chopped
125 g (4½ oz/½ cup) ricotta cheese
100 ml (3½ fl oz) pouring cream
2 teaspoons finely grated lemon zest
100 g (3½ oz/1 cup) grated parmesan
  cheese
1 handful basil, chopped
small basil leaves, to serve
parmesan cheese shavings, to serve

Cook the penne in a large saucepan
of boiling salted water until al dente.
Drain, reserving 125 ml (4 fl oz/½ cup)
of the cooking water.

Meanwhile, to make the sauce, put
zucchini, garlic and chilli in a small
processor fitted with the metal blade
and whizz in short bursts for about
30 seconds, or until finely chopped.
Add the ricotta, cream, lemon zest,
parmesan and chopped basil. Season
with salt and freshly ground black
pepper, then process for 20 seconds,
or until smooth.

Pour sauce over the hot pasta, adding
enough of the reserved cooking water
to make a coating consistency. Serve
immediately, topped with small basil
leaves and parmesan shavings.

Serves 4

Tip: Prepare the sauce just prior to
serving. It is not suitable for freezing.

Rice noodles with beef and black beans

300 g (10½ oz) rump steak
1 garlic clove, crushed
3 tablespoons oyster sauce
2 tablespoons sugar
2 tablespoons soy sauce
100 ml (3½ fl oz) black bean sauce
2 teaspoons cornflour (cornstarch)
¾ teaspoon sesame oil
1.2 kg (2 lb 11 oz) fresh or 600 g
   (1 lb 5 oz) dried flat rice noodles
1½ tablespoons oil
2 red capsicums (peppers), sliced
1 green capsicum (pepper), sliced
1 handful coriander (cilantro) leaves

Cut steak across the grain into thin slices and put it in a bowl with garlic, oyster sauce, sugar, soy sauce, black bean sauce, cornflour and sesame oil. Mix everything together, making sure the slices are well coated.

Soak dried rice noodles, if using, in boiling water for about 10 minutes, or until they are opaque and soft. If your noodles are particularly dry, they may need a little longer. Then drain.

Heat oil in a wok or frying pan. Add capsicums and stir-fry for 1–2 minutes until they start to soften. Add the meat mixture and cook for 1 minute. Add the noodles and toss everything together well. Continue cooking until the meat is cooked through and all the ingredients are hot. Toss in coriander leaves and stir once before turning off the heat. Serve at once.

Serves 4

Bucatini all'amatriciana

100 ml (3½ fl oz) extra virgin olive oil
1 red onion, finely chopped
75 g (2½ oz) pancetta, smoked
  pancetta or guanciale
1 tablespoon chopped rosemary
  leaves
2 garlic cloves, chopped
1 large dried chilli (optional)
200 ml (7 fl oz) red wine
800 g (1 lb 12 oz) tinned chopped
  tomatoes
500 g (1 lb 2 oz) bucatini
grated parmesan cheese, to serve

Heat olive oil in a saucepan and cook the onion and pancetta over low heat until they are soft and caramelized, being careful they don't burn. Add the rosemary, garlic and chilli and cook until garlic is light brown.

Add the red wine and bring to the boil, scraping the bottom of the saucepan for anything that may be stuck to it, as this will give flavour to the sauce. When the wine has reduced, add the tomatoes and simmer gently for about 10 minutes, or until the sauce has reduced and thickened. Remove chilli.

Cook the pasta in a large saucepan of boiling salted water until it is al dente. Drain briefly, allowing some of the water to remain clinging to the pasta, then mix with the sauce. Serve with the parmesan sprinkled over the top.

Serves 4

Carrot and pumpkin risotto

90 g (3¼ oz) unsalted butter
1 onion, finely chopped
400 g (14 oz) pumpkin (winter
  squash), peeled, seeded and finely
  chopped to give 300 g (10½ oz/
  2 cups)
3 carrots, chopped
2 litres (70 fl oz/8 cups) vegetable or
  chicken stock
440 g (15½ oz/2 cups) risotto rice
90 g (3¼ oz/1 cup) shaved pecorino
  or parmesan cheese
¼ teaspoon freshly grated nutmeg
½ teaspoon thyme leaves

Heat 60 g (2¼ oz) of the butter in a
large heavy-based saucepan. Add the
onion and sauté over medium heat
for 2–3 minutes, or until beginning to
soften. Add the pumpkin and carrot
and cook for 6–8 minutes, or until
tender. Mash the mixture slightly using
a potato masher.

Meanwhile, pour the stock into a
separate saucepan and bring to the
boil. Reduce the heat, then cover and
keep at simmering point.

Add the rice to the vegetables
and cook for 1–2 minutes, stirring
constantly, until the grains are
translucent and heated through.
Add 125 ml (4 fl oz/½ cup) of the
simmering stock and cook, stirring
constantly, until all the stock has been
absorbed. Continue adding the stock,
125 ml (4 fl oz/½ cup) at a time,
stirring constantly and making sure
it has been absorbed before adding
more. Cook for 20–25 minutes, or
until rice is tender and creamy; you
may need slightly less or more stock.
Remove from the heat, then add the
remaining butter, cheese, nutmeg and
thyme. Season with freshly ground
black pepper and stir well. Cover and
leave for 5 minutes before serving.

Serves 6

Grilled asparagus and zucchini lasagne

500 g (1 lb 2 oz) asparagus spears,
    trimmed
500 g (1 lb 2 oz) zucchini (courgettes),
    sliced lengthways into 5 mm
    (¼ inch) thick ribbons
2 tablespoons olive oil
6 large (20 x 15 cm/8 x 6 inch) fresh
    lasagne sheets
150 g (5½ oz/1 cup) grated
    mozzarella cheese

White sauce
500 ml (17 fl oz/2 cups) milk
50 g (1¾ oz) butter
50 g (1¾ oz) plain (all-purpose) flour
125 ml (4 fl oz/½ cup) pouring cream
pinch of grated nutmeg

Heat a grill (broiler) to medium. Gently toss the asparagus and zucchini with the oil. Spread on a baking tray and grill (broil) in batches for 2–3 minutes, turning during cooking. Cool, then cut the asparagus into shorter lengths.

Bring a large saucepan of salted water to the boil. Add the lasagne sheets and stir gently with a wooden spoon. Boil for about 5–7 minutes, or until al dente. Drain, then carefully lay the sheets on a clean tea towel to dry.

Preheat oven to 180°C (350°F/Gas 4). To make the white sauce, gently heat the milk in a small saucepan and set aside. In another saucepan, melt the butter and stir in the flour. Cook over medium heat, stirring with a wooden spoon, for 3 minutes. Gradually add the milk and stir for 5 minutes, or until the sauce boils and thickens. Remove from the heat and stir in the cream and nutmeg. Season with salt and white pepper.

Lay two pasta sheets in a lightly oiled 20 x 30 cm (8 x 12 inch) baking dish and spread with a little white sauce. Top with a layer of grilled vegetables, then spread with more white sauce. Repeat to form another two layers, then sprinkle with mozzarella. Bake for 45 minutes, or until golden brown.

Serves 4

Spicy chicken stir-fry

4 dried shiitake mushrooms
250 g (9 oz) flat rice stick noodles
oil spray
1 red onion, cut into thin wedges
2 garlic cloves, crushed
2 x 2 cm (3/4 x 3/4 inch) piece fresh
  ginger, thinly sliced
1 tablespoon chilli jam
400 g (14 oz) boneless, skinless
  chicken breast, cut into strips
1/2 red capsicum (pepper), cut into thin
  strips
1 bunch (800 g/1 lb 12 oz) Chinese
  broccoli (gai larn), cut into 5 cm
  (2 inch) lengths
115 g (4 oz) fresh or tinned baby corn,
  halved on the diagonal
150 g (5 1/2 oz/1 1/2 cups) snowpeas
  (mangetout), halved on the diagonal
4 tablespoons soy sauce
2 tablespoons mirin (Japanese
  cooking wine)
1 large handful coriander (cilantro)
  leaves

Place the mushrooms in a heatproof bowl. Cover with 374 ml (13 fl oz/ 1 1/2 cups) boiling water and stand for 15 minutes. Drain, reserving the liquid and squeezing out any excess liquid. Remove the stalks and thinly slice the caps. Place the noodles in a heatproof bowl, pour over boiling water to cover and let stand for 5 minutes, or until tender. Drain.

Meanwhile, heat a non-stick wok or large frying pan over a high heat and spray with oil. Add onion and cook for 2–3 minutes. Add garlic, ginger and chilli jam; cook for 1 minute, adding 1–2 tablespoons of reserved mushroom liquid.

Add chicken and cook for 5 minutes, or until almost cooked through. Add the capsicum, Chinese broccoli, corn, snowpeas, mushrooms and 3 tablespoons reserved mushroom liquid. Stir-fry for 3 minutes, or until vegetables are tender. Add the soy sauce, mirin, coriander and noodles and season with ground white pepper. Toss until well combined, then serve.

Serves 4

Note: Dried shiitake mushrooms, chilli jam and mirin are readily available in supermarkets and Asian food stores.

Pasta Alfredo

500 g (1 lb 2 oz) pasta (see Note)
90 g (3¼ oz) butter
150 g (5½ oz/1½ cups) grated
  parmesan cheese
315 ml (10¾ fl oz/1¼ cups) pouring
  cream
3 tablespoons chopped parsley

Cook pasta in a large pan of rapidly boiling salted water until al dente. Drain well and return to the pan to keep warm.

While the pasta is cooking, melt the butter in a saucepan over low heat. Add the parmesan and cream and bring to the boil, stirring constantly. Reduce the heat and simmer, stirring, until the sauce has thickened slightly. Add the parsley, season to taste, and stir until well combined.

Add the sauce to the pasta and toss well so the sauce coats the pasta. Garnish with chopped herbs or sprigs of fresh herbs such as thyme.

Serves 4–6

Note: Traditionally, fettucine is used with this sauce, but you can try any pasta. Try to time the sauce so it is ready just as the pasta is cooked.

Orecchiette with broccoli

750 g (1 lb 10 oz) broccoli, cut into
  florets
450 g (1 lb) orecchiette
3 tablespoons extra virgin olive oil
1/2 teaspoon dried chilli flakes
30 g (1 oz/1/3 cup) grated pecorino
  or parmesan cheese

Blanch broccoli in a large saucepan of boiling salted water for 5 minutes, or until just tender. Remove with a slotted spoon, drain well and return the water to the boil.

Cook the pasta in the boiling water until al dente. Drain well and return to the pan to keep warm.

Meanwhile, heat the oil in a heavy-based frying pan over medium heat. Add the chilli flakes and broccoli and cook, stirring, for 5 minutes, or until the broccoli is well coated and beginning to break apart. Season. Add to the pasta, stir through the cheese and serve.

Serves 6

Spaghetti carbonara

500 g (1 lb 2 oz) dried spaghetti
8 rindless bacon slices (about 450 g/
  1 lb)
2 teaspoons olive oil
4 eggs, lightly beaten
50 g (1¾ oz/½ cup) freshly grated
  parmesan cheese
300 ml (10½ fl oz/1¼ cups) pouring
  cream
finely snipped chives, to garnish
  (optional)

Cook spaghetti in a large saucepan of boiling salted water until al dente, then drain and return to the pan.

Meanwhile, cut the bacon into thin strips. Heat the olive oil in a heavy-based frying pan, add the bacon and cook over medium heat, stirring often, for 5 minutes, or until crisp. Remove and drain on paper towels.

Working quickly, whisk the eggs, parmesan and cream in a bowl until combined. Add the bacon, then pour the mixture over the hot pasta in the pan. Toss to coat the pasta with the sauce and cook over a very low heat for 1 minute, stirring, or until slightly thickened. Take care not to overheat the sauce, or the eggs will scramble.

Season with freshly ground black pepper. Divide among warmed bowls.

Serves 6

Tandoori chicken skewers

1½ tablespoons tandoori spice
  powder
125 g (4½ oz/½ cup) low-fat plain
  yoghurt
1 tablespoon lemon juice
4 (200 g/7 oz) skinless chicken fillets,
  cut into 2 cm (¾ inch) strips
300 g (10½ oz/1½ cups) basmati rice
2 teaspoons oil
1 small onion, finely diced
2 garlic cloves, crushed
1 teaspoon ginger, finely grated
½ teaspoon ground turmeric
1 teaspoon cumin seeds
4 bruised cardamom pods
1 stick cinnamon
500 ml (17 fl oz/ 2 cups) chicken
  stock
2 tablespoons currants
oil spray
mango chutney, lemon wedges and
  coriander (cilantro) leaves, to serve

Soak 8 bamboo skewers in cold water for 30 minutes. Place the spice powder, yoghurt, lemon juice and chicken in a non-metallic bowl. Mix well to combine, then cover and refrigerate for 2 hours.

For the pilaf, rinse the rice under cold water until it runs clear. Heat the oil over a medium heat in a saucepan, add the onion, garlic, ginger, turmeric and cumin seeds. Cook for 5 minutes, or until softened. Add rice, cardamom, cinnamon and chicken stock.

Bring to the boil, reduce the heat to low, cover and cook for 12 minutes. Remove from heat, add the currants and stir through. Season well with salt and freshly ground black pepper and set aside, covered, for 10 minutes before serving.

Meanwhile, weave chicken pieces onto the skewers so they are evenly distributed, but not too close together. Heat a chargrill pan or frying pan over medium heat and spray with oil. Add skewers, and cook for 12–15 minutes, turning, so that chicken cooks evenly. Serve the skewers on the rice pilaf with mango chutney, lemon wedges and coriander leaves.

Serves 4

Kedgeree

600 g (1 lb 5 oz) smoked haddock
50 g (1¾ oz) butter
1 onion, finely chopped
2 teaspoons curry powder
1 teaspoon ground cumin
1 teaspoon ground coriander
2 teaspoons seeded and finely sliced
  green chilli
200 g (7 oz/1 cup) basmati rice
660 ml (22½ fl oz) chicken or fish
  stock
1 cinnamon stick
80 ml (2½ fl oz/⅓ cup) pouring cream
2 hard-boiled eggs, finely chopped
2 tablespoons chopped parsley
2 tablespoons chopped coriander
  (cilantro)

Poach the haddock in a large shallow frying pan, skin-side up, cover with boiling water and simmer very gently for about 10 minutes. The fish is cooked when the flesh can be flaked easily with a fork. Drain and pat dry with paper towels. Remove the skin and flake into bite-size chunks.

Heat the butter in a large saucepan and add the onion. Cook until golden, then add the curry powder, cumin, coriander and chilli. Cook, stirring, for 1 minute. Add rice, stir well, then pour in the stock and add cinnamon stick. Cover tightly and simmer over gentle heat for about 12 minutes, or until the rice is tender.

Remove the cinnamon stick and gently stir in the haddock. Fold through the cream, chopped egg and the herbs. Season and serve immediately.

Serves 4

Penne all'arrabbiata

2 tablespoons olive oil
2 large garlic cloves, thinly sliced
1–2 dried chillies
800 g (1 lb 12 oz) tinned tomatoes
400 g (14 oz) penne
1 basil sprig, torn into pieces

Cook the pasta in a large saucepan of boiling salted water until al dente. Drain well and return to the pan to keep warm.

Meanwhile, heat oil in a saucepan over a low heat. Add the garlic and chillies and cook until the garlic is light golden brown. Turn the chillies over during cooking so both sides are infused with oil. Add tomatoes and season with salt. Cook gently, breaking up tomatoes with a wooden spoon, for 20–30 minutes, or until the sauce is rich and thick.

Add the basil to the sauce and toss with the pasta. Season to taste.

Serves 4

Cotelli with spring vegetables

500 g (17 oz) cotelli
310 g (11 oz/2 cups) frozen peas
310 g (11 oz/2 cups) frozen broad
  beans, blanched and peeled
90 ml (3 fl oz/⅓ cup) olive oil
6 spring onions (scallions), cut into
  3 cm (1¼ inch) pieces
2 cloves garlic, finely chopped
250 ml (8 fl oz/1 cup) chicken stock
12 thin fresh asparagus spears,
  cut into 5 cm (2 inch) lengths
½ teaspoon finely grated lemon zest
60 ml (2 fl oz/½ cup) lemon juice
shaved parmesan cheese, to serve

Cook the cotelli in a large saucepan of rapidly boiling salted water until al dente. Drain; return to pan. Cook the peas in a saucepan of boiling water for 1–2 minutes, until tender. Remove with a slotted spoon and plunge into cold water. Add the broad beans to the saucepan, cook for 1–2 minutes, then drain and plunge into cold water. Remove and slip the skins off.

Heat 2 tablespoons oil in a frying pan. Add the spring onion and garlic, and cook over medium heat for 2 minutes, or until softened. Pour in the stock and cook for 5 minutes, or until slightly reduced. Add the asparagus and cook for 3–4 minutes, until bright green and just tender. Stir in the peas and broad beans and cook for 2–3 minutes, or until heated through.

Toss remaining oil through the pasta, then add the vegetable mixture, lemon zest and lemon juice. Season to taste with salt and cracked black pepper and toss together well. Divide among four bowls. Top with shaved parmesan, if desired.

Serves 4

Spaghettini with garlic and oil

500 g (1 lb 2 oz) spaghettini
90 ml (3 fl oz) extra virgin olive oil
5 garlic cloves, crushed
pinch of dried chilli flakes
2 tablespoons finely chopped flat-leaf (Italian) parsley
grated pecorino cheese, to serve

Cook the pasta in a large saucepan of boiling salted water until al dente.

Meanwhile, heat the oil in a large frying pan over very low heat. Add the garlic and chilli flakes and fry gently for about 2 minutes, or until the garlic has softened but not browned. Remove from the heat.

Drain the pasta briefly, leaving some of the water clinging to the pasta. Add the hot pasta and parsley to the frying pan and toss to coat. Taste for seasoning and serve at once with the grated pecorino.

Serves 4

Meat & Poultry

Lamb kebabs with mint buttermilk sauce

5 garlic cloves, chopped
5 cm (2 inch) piece ginger, chopped
3 green chillies, chopped and
  deseeded
1 onion, chopped
3 tablespoons Greek-style yoghurt
3 tablespoons coriander (cilantro)
  leaves
500 g (1 lb 2 oz) minced (ground)
  lamb
red onion rings and lemon wedges,
  to serve

Mint buttermilk sauce
1 teaspoon cumin seeds
1 small handful mint leaves, chopped
½ cup coriander (cilantro) leaves,
  chopped
2 cm (¾ inch) piece ginger, chopped
2 green chillies, chopped
310 ml (10¾ fl oz/1¼ cups)
  Greek-style yoghurt
310 ml (10¾ fl oz/1¼ cups) buttermilk
sea salt

Combine garlic, ginger, chilli, onion, yoghurt and coriander leaves in a food processor and process to a thick, smooth paste. Season, then combine with the lamb and mix well. Divide into 16 pieces and shape into oval patties. Cover and chill for 20 minutes.

Meanwhile, make the mint buttermilk sauce. Dry-fry cumin seeds in a small, heavy-based frying pan over low heat, for 2 minutes or until aromatic. Cool, then grind the seeds to a fine powder using an electric spice grinder or a mortar and pestle. Combine the mint, coriander, ginger and chilli in a food processor or blender then process or blend until a smooth paste forms. Or, chop mixture to a fine paste using a large, sharp knife. Add the yoghurt and buttermilk to the mixture in the food processor, then process until well combined and smooth. Season with sea salt and freshly ground black pepper, then stir in the cumin.

Heat the grill (broiler) to high. Thread four patties onto each of four metal skewers. Grill (broil) for 7 minutes, or until brown. Turn and cook the other side for 6–7 minutes, or until browned and cooked through. Serve with the mint buttermilk sauce, red onion rings and lemon wedges.

Serves 4

Chicken breast with Asian greens and soy mushroom sauce

2 large dried shiitake mushrooms
4 tablespoons boiling water
2 tablespoons light soy sauce
2 tablespoons Chinese rice wine
½ tablespoon sesame oil
1 tablespoon finely sliced fresh ginger
4 x 200 g (7 oz) boneless, skinless chicken breasts
450 g (1 lb) bok choy (pak choy), ends removed and cut lengthways into quarters
250 ml (9 fl oz/1 cup) chicken stock
1 tablespoon cornflour (cornstarch)

Soak the dried mushrooms in the boiling water for 20 minutes. Drain, reserving the soaking liquid. Discard the stalks and finely slice the caps.

Combine the soy sauce, rice wine, sesame oil and ginger in a non-metallic dish. Add the chicken and turn to coat. Cover and marinate in the refrigerator for 1 hour.

Line a steamer with baking paper and punch holes in the paper. Place the chicken on top, reserving the marinade. Cover steamer and place it over a wok or saucepan of boiling water for 6 minutes, then turn the chicken over and steam for a further 6 minutes. Place bok choy on top of the chicken. Steam for 2–3 minutes.

Meanwhile, put reserved marinade, mushrooms and the soaking liquid in a small saucepan. Bring to the boil. In a small bowl, mix enough stock to the cornflour to make a smooth paste. Add paste and remaining stock to pan and stir over a medium heat for 2 minutes, or until sauce thickens.

Arrange the chicken fillets and bok choy on serving plates, pour the sauce over the top and serve with steamed rice.

Serves 4

Coriander pork with fresh pineapple

400 g (14 oz) pork loin or fillet,
 trimmed
¼ pineapple
1 tablespoon vegetable oil
4 garlic cloves, chopped
4 spring onions (scallions), chopped
1 tablespoon fish sauce
1 tablespoon lime juice
a large handful of coriander (cilantro)
 leaves
a large handful of chopped mint
steamed rice, to serve

Partially freeze the pork until it is just firm, then slice thinly. Cut the skin off the pineapple, then cut the flesh into bite-sized pieces.

Heat the oil in a wok or heavy-based frying pan. Add the garlic and spring onion and cook over medium–high heat for 1 minute. Remove from wok.

Heat wok to very hot, then add pork in batches and stir-fry for 2–3 minutes, or until just cooked.

Return the garlic, spring onion and all the pork to the wok and add the pineapple, fish sauce and lime juice. Toss together, then cook for 1 minute, or until pineapple is heated through.

Toss coriander and mint through and serve immediately, with steamed rice.

Serves 4

Grilled polenta with sausage and tomato sauce

1 tablespoon salt
300 g (10½ oz) coarse-grain polenta
50 g (1¾ oz) butter
50 g (1¾ oz) parmesan cheese,
  grated, plus extra to serve

Sausage and tomato sauce
3 tablespoons olive oil
8 firm Italian pork sausages
1 onion, halved and sliced
2 garlic cloves, chopped
200 ml (7 fl oz) red wine
400 g (14 oz) tinned tomatoes

Bring 1.5 litres (52 fl oz/6 cups) water to the boil in a deep heavy-based saucepan. Add salt, then polenta in a gentle stream, whisking vigorously. Reduce the heat immediately so the water is simmering; keep stirring for 30 seconds to prevent lumps. Cook for 40 minutes, stirring frequently to prevent it sticking to the pan. Finished polenta should drop from the spoon in thick lumps. Stir in the butter and parmesan. Pour polenta onto a plate. Leave to cool at room temperature.

To make the sauce, heat the oil in a frying pan over medium–high heat. Cook the sausages, browning on all sides, then remove. Cook the onion until softened, scraping the fat from the bottom of the pan. Add garlic, cook for a few more minutes, then pour in the wine. Cook for 5 minutes, or until the liquid has reduced and thickened. Add tomatoes and, when the sauce starts to thicken, add the sausages, stirring frequently. Season with salt and pepper.

Preheat a chargrill pan or barbecue grill. Cut the polenta into triangles, brush with oil and grill for 3 minutes on each side. Spoon the sauce over the sausages and sprinkle the polenta with parmesan.

Serves 4

Beef salad with sweet and sour cucumber

2 Lebanese (short) cucumbers
4 teaspoons caster (superfine) sugar
4 tablespoons red wine vinegar
1 tablespoon oil
2 large or 4 small fillet steaks, cut into
  strips
8 spring onions (scallions), cut into
  pieces
2 garlic cloves, crushed
2 tablespoons ginger, grated
2 tablespoons soy sauce
4 handfuls mixed lettuce leaves

Halve cucumber lengthways, then thinly slice and put in a colander. Sprinkle with a little salt and leave for 10 minutes. This will draw out any excess moisture.

Put 2 teaspoons each of the sugar and vinegar in a bowl and stir until the sugar dissolves. Rinse off salt, then drain the cucumber very thoroughly and dab with a paper towel to soak up any leftover moisture. Combine cucumber and vinegar mixture.

Heat half the oil in a frying pan until it is smoking. Add half the steak and fry for 1 minute. Remove from the pan and repeat with the remaining oil and steak. Return to the same pan, then add the spring onion and fry for another minute. Add garlic and ginger, toss everything around at once, then add soy sauce and remaining sugar and vinegar. Cook until sauce turns sticky. Quickly remove from the heat.

Put a handful of lettuce leaves on four plates and divide the beef among them. Scatter some cucumber on the beef and serve the rest on the side.

Serves 4

Marinated stuffed chicken wings

8 large chicken wings
potato flour or cornflour (cornstarch),
   for coating
vegetable oil, for deep-frying
2 spring onions (scallions), sliced
   on the diagonal

Marinade
1½ tablespoons light soy sauce
1 tablespoon honey
2 teaspoons grated fresh ginger
2 garlic cloves, finely chopped

Filling
180 g (6 oz) minced (ground) pork
60 g (2¼ oz/⅓ cup) chopped water
   chestnuts
2 tablespoons chopped coriander
   (cilantro) leaves
2 teaspoons cornflour (cornstarch)
3 teaspoons grated fresh ginger
2 garlic cloves, chopped
2 teaspoons oyster sauce
2 teaspoons light soy sauce
¼ teaspoon sesame oil

Prepare the chicken by cutting down the middle through the loose skin, slightly closer to the drumstick. Twist and break the joint between one small drumstick and the wing, then cut through the joint. Take the wing section and, using a small sharp knife, gently scrape the meat away from the bone, being careful not to break the skin. Pull the bone away and discard. Carefully remove the bone from the small drumsticks by scraping the meat away from the bone. Put all the chicken pieces in a large bowl.

Combine all the marinade ingredients in a bowl. Add the chicken and mix well. Cover and marinate for at least 1 hour, or preferably overnight.

To make the filling, combine all the ingredients. Spoon into the deboned wings and drumsticks, and lightly coat in potato flour. Half-fill a wok with oil and heat to 170°C (325°F), or until a cube of bread dropped in the oil browns in 20 seconds. Cook the chicken in batches for 8 minutes, or until cooked through. Don't have the oil too hot, otherwise the chicken will brown too quickly and the centre won't cook. Drain on paper towels.

Garnish with spring onion and serve with rice and green vegetables.

Serves 4

Fennel roasted pork belly with apple sauce

2 kg (4 lb 8 oz) piece of pork belly on the bone, cut from the thick end of the belly
olive oil, for brushing
2 teaspoons fennel seeds
a large pinch of ground cloves
1 tablespoon sea salt flakes
6 onions, cut in half

Apple sauce
4 Granny Smith apples, peeled, cored and roughly chopped
1 tablespoon caster (superfine) sugar
2 cloves
1 cinnamon stick
1–2 teaspoons lemon juice, to taste

Preheat the oven to 200°C (400°F/Gas 6). Score the pork skin in a series of 1 cm (½ inch) parallel lines, cutting 5 mm (¼ inch) into the fat. Rub a little olive oil all over the pork skin. Using a mortar and pestle, coarsely grind the fennel seeds. Place in a bowl with the cloves and sea salt, then rub over the pork skin and into the incisions.

Place the pork on a rack in a roasting tin and pour 500 ml (17 fl oz/2 cups) boiling water into the tin. Arrange the onion halves around the pork. Roast for 30 minutes, or until the pork skin is golden. Reduce the oven to 180°C (350°F/Gas 4). Roast for 2 hours, or until the juices run clear when pierced through the thickest part. Remove from the oven, cover loosely with foil and rest for 20 minutes.

Meanwhile, make apple sauce. Put the apples, sugar, cloves, cinnamon stick and 125 ml (4 fl oz/½ cup) water in a small saucepan. Stir to dissolve the sugar, then cover and simmer over low heat for 10 minutes, or until the apple is very soft. Discard the cloves and cinnamon. Mash the apple and stir in lemon juice to taste.

Carve the pork, with the skin. Serve with the roasted onion halves, with the apple sauce passed separately.

Serves 6–8

Beef cheeks, olive and red onion pies

Filling

2 tablespoons olive oil

500 g (1 lb 2 oz) trimmed beef cheeks (have your butcher do this), cut into 1.5 cm (⅝ inch) chunks

1 onion, finely chopped

50 g (1¾ oz) pancetta, finely chopped

2 garlic cloves, crushed

1 tablespoon tomato paste (concentrated purée)

250 ml (9 fl oz/1 cup) red wine

125 ml (4 fl oz/½ cup) beef stock

125 g (4½ oz/½ cup) tomato passata (puréed tomatoes)

1 teaspoon dried oregano

85 g (3 oz/½ cup) pitted green olives, roughly chopped

750 g (1 lb 10 oz) ready-made shortcrust pastry

1 egg, lightly beaten

To make the filling, heat half the oil in a large saucepan and cook the beef cheeks in batches over high heat for 5 minutes, turning to brown all over. Remove and set aside. Reduce heat to medium–low, add the remaining oil and cook the onion, pancetta and garlic for 3–4 minutes, or until the onion has softened. Return the beef to the pan, stir in the remaining filling ingredients, then cover and simmer over low heat for 50–60 minutes, or until the beef is tender. Season with sea salt and pepper. Remove the lid and cook for a further 30 minutes, or until the sauce has reduced. Set aside to cool.

Preheat oven to 180°C (350°F/Gas 4) and place a baking tray in the oven. Grease 24 patty pans or mini muffin holes measuring 5 cm (2 inches) across the top. Roll pastry thinly and cut 24 squares measuring 10 cm (4 inches) across. Repeat with a 5 cm (2 inch) round cutter. Fit the squares in each hole and fill with the cooled filling. Dampen edges of the rounds and place over the filling to seal the pies. Trim excess pastry. Brush the tops with beaten egg and cut three slits in the top of each one. Bake on the hot baking tray for 25 minutes, or until golden. Cool slightly before removing from the pans.

Makes 24

Italian meatballs with tomato sauce

Meatballs
185 ml (6 fl oz/³/₄ cup) olive oil
1 onion, finely chopped
75 g (2½ oz/½ cup) pine nuts, roughly chopped
3 garlic cloves, crushed
2 large handfuls of parsley, roughly chopped
3 tablespoons roughly chopped basil or rosemary
2 teaspoons fennel seeds, ground
50 g (1³/₄ oz/²/₃ cup) fresh breadcrumbs
250 g (9 oz/1 cup) ricotta cheese
3 tablespoons grated parmesan cheese
grated zest of 1 large lemon
1 egg
500 g (1 lb 2 oz) minced (ground) pork

Tomato sauce
800 g (1 lb 12 oz) ripe, firm tomatoes, peeled and chopped, or 2 x 400 g (14 oz) tins chopped tomatoes
100 ml (3½ fl oz) red wine

To make the meatballs, heat half the oil in a frying pan. Add the onion and pine nuts and sauté for 5–6 minutes, or until the onion has softened and the pine nuts are light golden. Add the garlic and cook for a few minutes more, then set aside to cool. Combine the remaining meatball ingredients in a bowl. Add the cooled onion mixture, season with sea salt and freshly ground black pepper and mix until well combined. Fry a piece of the mixture to check the seasoning, and adjust, if necessary. Refrigerate for at least 30 minutes or overnight to allow the flavours to develop.

Roll the meatball mixture into walnut-sized balls. Heat the remaining oil in a large frying pan. Cook the meatballs in batches for 8 minutes, or until golden brown all over, turning occasionally. Remove and set aside.

Put the tomatoes and wine in a large saucepan, season with sea salt and freshly ground black pepper, and simmer for 5 minutes. Carefully add meatballs to the sauce. Reduce heat to a gentle simmer, then cover and cook a further 10 minutes. Allow to stand for 10 minutes before serving.

Serves 4

Chicken with apricots and honey

40 g (1½ oz) unsalted butter
1 teaspoon ground cinnamon
1 teaspoon ground ginger
a pinch of cayenne pepper
½ teaspoon freshly ground black
  pepper
4 x 175 g (6 oz) boneless, skinless
  chicken breasts, trimmed
1 onion, thinly sliced
250 ml (9 fl oz/1 cup) chicken stock
6 coriander (cilantro) sprigs, tied in a
  bunch, plus extra sprigs, to garnish
500 g (1 lb 2 oz) apricots, halved and
  stones removed
2 tablespoons honey
2 tablespoons slivered almonds,
  toasted
steamed couscous, to serve

Melt the butter in a large frying pan. Add the spices and stir over low heat for 1 minute, or until fragrant. Increase the heat to medium and add chicken breasts. Cook for 1 minute on each side, taking care not to let the spices burn. Remove chicken from the pan.

Add the onion to the pan and sauté for 5 minutes, or until softened. Return the chicken to the pan, add the stock and tied coriander sprigs and season with sea salt and freshly ground black pepper. Reduce heat to low, cover and simmer for 5 minutes, turning the chicken once.

Transfer chicken to a serving dish, cover and let rest for a few minutes.

Meanwhile, put the apricots, cut side down, into the pan juices and drizzle with the honey. Cover and simmer for 7–8 minutes, turning the apricots after 5 minutes. Remove the coriander sprigs and discard.

Spoon the apricots and sauce over the chicken. Scatter the almonds over and garnish with a few extra coriander sprigs. Serve with steamed couscous served separately.

Serves 4

Potato gnocchi with sage and pancetta sauce

1 kg (2 lb 4 oz) floury potatoes, such as Russet (Idaho) or King Edward, unpeeled and pricked all over
200 g (7 oz/scant 1²/₃ cups) plain (all-purpose) flour, plus extra, for kneading

Sage and pancetta sauce
20 g (³/₄ oz) unsalted butter
80 g (2³/₄ oz) pancetta or bacon slices, cut into thin strips
8 very small sage or basil leaves
150 ml (5 fl oz) thick (double/heavy) cream
50 g (1³/₄ oz/¹/₂ cup) shaved parmesan cheese

Preheat the oven to 180°C (350°F/ Gas 4). Bake the potatoes in a non-stick roasting tin for 1 hour, or until tender. Cool for 15 minutes, then peel and put through a food processor. Gradually stir in the flour. When the mixture gets too firm, work the flour in with your hands. Transfer to a floured surface and knead gently. Work in enough flour to give a soft, pliable dough. Divide into six portions. Taking one portion at a time, roll into a rope 1.5 cm (⁵/₈ inch) thick. Cut into 1.5 cm (⁵/₈ inch) lengths. Press your finger into a piece of dough to form a concave shape, then roll the outer surface over the tines of a fork. Fold outer lips into the centre. Cook, in batches, in a large saucepan of salted water for 2 minutes, or until gnocchi rise to the surface. Remove with a slotted spoon and place in a greased baking tray.

Preheat the oven to 200°C (400°F/ Gas 6). To make the sauce, melt butter in a frying pan and fry pancetta until crisp, drain and set aside. Fry sage until crisp, drain and set aside. Add cream, season and simmer for 5–10 minutes, or until thickened, then pover gnocchi and mix through. Scatter with the parmesan, pancetta and sage. Bake for 10–15 minutes, or until cheese is golden.

Serves 4

Shepherd's pie

60 ml (2 fl oz/¼ cup) olive oil
1 large onion, finely chopped
2 garlic cloves, crushed
2 celery stalks, finely chopped
3 carrots, diced
2 bay leaves
1 tablespoon thyme, chopped
1 kg (2 lb 4 oz) good-quality minced (ground) lamb
1½ tablespoons plain (all-purpose) flour
125 ml (4 fl oz/½ cup) dry red wine
2 tablespoons tomato paste (concentrated purée)
400 g (14 oz) tin crushed tomatoes
1.5 kg (3 lb 5 oz) floury potatoes (such as Desiree), cut into even-sized pieces
60 ml(2 fl oz/¼ cup) milk
100 g (3½ oz) butter
½ teaspoon ground nutmeg

Heat 2 tablespoons of the oil over medium heat in a large heavy-based pan and cook onion for 3–4 minutes, or until softened. Add garlic, celery, carrot, bay leaves and thyme and cook for 2–3 minutes. Transfer to a bowl; remove bay leaves.

Add the remaining oil to the same pan, add the mince and cook over high heat for 5–6 minutes, or until it changes colour. Mix in the flour, cook for 1 minute, then pour in the red wine and cook for 2–3 minutes. Return vegetables to pan with tomato paste and crushed tomato. Reduce heat, cover, and simmer for 45 minutes, stirring occasionally. Season, then transfer to a shallow 3 litre (12 cup) ovenproof dish and leave to cool. Preheat oven to 180°C (350°F/Gas 4).

Meanwhile, boil the potatoes in salted water over medium heat for about 25 minutes, or until tender. Drain, then mash with milk and butter until smooth. Season with nutmeg and black pepper. Spoon over mince and fluff with a fork. Bake for 30 minutes, or until golden and crusty.

Serves 6

Braised sausages with puy lentils

1 tablespoon olive oil
100 g (3½ oz) pancetta, cut into
  cubes
2 red onions, finely chopped
12 Toulouse sausages, or any good-
  quality fresh pork sausages
2 garlic cloves, bruised
2 thyme sprigs
300 g (10½ oz/1½ cups) puy lentils or
  tiny blue-green lentils
750 ml (26 fl oz/3 cups) tinned
  chicken consommé
150 g (5½ oz) baby English spinach
  leaves, finely chopped
crusty bread, to serve

Heat the olive oil in a large heavy-based frying pan. Add the pancetta and sauté over medium–high heat for 5–6 minutes, or until browned. Using a slotted spoon, remove the pancetta and place in a bowl.

Add the onion to the pan and sauté over medium heat for 5–6 minutes, or until softened and only lightly browned. Remove the onion and add to the pancetta.

Fry the sausages in the same pan, in batches if necessary, for 10 minutes, or until deep golden, turning often.

Return the pancetta and onion to the pan, add the garlic, thyme and lentils and stir together well. Pour in the consommé and bring to the boil. Reduce the heat, cover and simmer for 30–35 minutes, or until the lentils are tender.

Stir in the spinach and season to taste with sea salt and freshly ground black pepper. Serve in warmed bowls with crusty bread.

Serves 4

Cheeseburgers with capsicum salsa

Capsicum salsa
2 red capsicums (peppers)
1 ripe tomato, finely chopped
1 small red onion, finely chopped
1 tablespoon olive oil
2 teaspoons red wine vinegar

1 kg (2 lb 4 oz) minced (ground) beef
1 small onion, finely chopped
2 tablespoons chopped flat-leaf (Italian) parsley
1 teaspoon dried oregano
1 tablespoon tomato paste (concentrated purée)
70 g (2½ oz) cheddar cheese
6 bread rolls
salad leaves, to serve

To make the salsa, quarter the capsicums, remove the seeds and membranes and cook on a hot, lightly oiled barbecue grill, skin-side down, until the skin blackens and blisters. Place in a plastic bag and leave to cool. Peel away the skin and dice the flesh. Combine with the tomato, onion, olive oil and vinegar and leave for at least 1 hour to let the flavours develop. Serve at room temperature.

Combine the ground beef, onion, herbs and tomato paste with your hands and season well. Divide into six portions and shape into patties. Cut cheese into small squares. Make a cavity in the top of each patty with your thumb. Place a piece of cheese in the cavity and smooth the mince over to enclose cheese completely.

Cook the patties on a hot, lightly oiled barbecue grill or flat plate for 4–5 minutes each side, turning once. Serve in rolls with salad leaves and capsicum salsa.

Serves 6

Variation: Use camembert, brie or a blue cheese instead of cheddar.

Paprika garlic chicken

1 kg (2 lb 4 oz) boneless, skinless
  chicken thighs
1 tablespoon paprika
2 tablespoons olive oil
8 garlic cloves, unpeeled
3 tablespoons brandy
125 ml (4 fl oz/½ cup) chicken stock
1 bay leaf
2 tablespoons chopped flat-leaf
  (Italian) parsley

Trim any excess fat from the chicken and cut thighs into thirds. Combine the paprika with some salt and pepper in a bowl, add the chicken and toss to coat.

Heat half the olive oil in a large frying pan over medium heat and cook the garlic for 1–2 minutes, until brown. Remove from the pan. Increase the heat to high and cook the chicken in batches for 5 minutes each batch, or until brown. Return all the chicken to the pan, add brandy and boil for 30 seconds, then add the stock and bay leaf. Reduce the heat, cover and simmer over low heat for 10 minutes.

Meanwhile, peel the garlic and put it in a mortar or small bowl. Add the parsley and pound with the pestle or crush with a fork to form a paste. Stir into the chicken, then cover and cook for 10 minutes, or until tender.

Serves 6

Lamb koftas in pitta bread

500 g (1 lb 2 oz) lean lamb, roughly
  chopped
1 onion, roughly chopped
1 large handful flat-leaf (Italian)
  parsley, roughly chopped
1 large handful mint, chopped
2 teaspoons lemon zest
1 teaspoons ground cumin
¼ teaspoon chilli powder
250 g (9 oz/1 cup) low-fat yoghurt
2 teaspoon lemon juice
oil spray
4 wholemeal (whole-wheat) pitta
  breads

Tabouleh
80g (3 oz/½ cup) bulgur (burghul)
2 vine-ripened tomatoes
1 telegraph (long) cucumber
1 small handful flat-leaf (Italian)
  parsley, chopped
2 French shallots, chopped
1 small handful mint
125 ml (4 fl oz/½ cup) ready-made
  fat-free dressing

Put the lamb and onion in a food
processor and process until smooth.
Add parsley, mint, lemon zest and
spices; process until well combined.
Divide mixture into 24 balls and place
on a tray. Cover and refrigerate for at
least 30 minutes.

Meanwhile, to make the tabouleh,
place the bulgur in a bowl. Cover
with boiling water and set aside for
10 minutes, or until softened. Drain,
then squeeze dry. Seed and chop the
tomatoes and cucumber and place
in a bowl. Add the parsley, mint and
shallots and stir through the dressing.

To make yoghurt dressing, combine
the yoghurt and lemon juice in a bowl.
Cover and refrigerate.

Heat a large, non-stick frying pan and
spray with the oil. Cook the lamb balls
in two batches, spraying with the oil
before each batch, until browned all
over and cooked through.

Preheat the oven to 350°F (180°C/
Gas 4). Cut the pitta pocket breads in
half, wrap in foil and place in the oven
for 10 minutes. Divide the tabouleh
between the pitta bread halves, add
3 kofta balls to each and top with the
yoghurt dressing.

Serves 4

Meat loaf

1 kg (2 lb 4 oz) lean minced (ground) beef
100 g (3½ oz/1 cup) dry breadcrumbs
1 onion, grated
2 teaspoons mixed dried herbs
1 egg
250 ml (8 fl oz/1 cup) tomato paste (concentrated puree)
2 tablespoons tomato sauce

Preheat the oven to 180°C (350°F/Gas 4). Place minced beef, breadcrumbs, onion, herbs, egg, tomato paste and some salt and pepper in a large bowl and mix together with your hands.

Shape the mixture into a firm loaf. Place in a greased baking dish and bake for 1 hour.

Carefully tip away any excess fat from the bottom of the baking dish. Spread the tomato sauce over the top of the meat loaf and bake for 30 minutes.

Serves 6

Mexican-style chicken with avocado salsa and cheese quesadillas

Avocado salsa
1 large avocado, diced
1 large tomato, seeded and diced
½ small red onion, diced
3 tablespoons finely chopped
   coriander (cilantro) leaves
   and stems
2 tablespoons extra virgin olive oil
1 tablespoon lime juice
3 teaspoons sweet chilli sauce
1 garlic clove, crushed

4 x 150 g (5½ oz) boneless, skinless
   chicken breasts
2 x 35 g (1¼ oz) packets taco
   seasoning
oil, for brushing

Cheese quesadillas
200 g (7 oz) grated cheddar cheese
1½ tablespoons finely chopped
   coriander (cilantro) leaves and stems
1 small red chilli, seeded and finely
   chopped
1 teaspoon sea salt
4 flour tortillas

Preheat a barbecue grill plate or chargrill pan to medium. Meanwhile, put all the avocado salsa ingredients in a small bowl, mix well and set aside.

Place chicken breasts between two sheets of plastic wrap and slightly flatten them with a rolling pin or mallet. Put them in a bowl with the taco seasoning and toss well to coat, pressing mixture in with your hands. Lightly brush the barbecue hotplate with oil, then cook chicken for about 5 minutes each side, or until golden and cooked through. Take the chicken off the heat and keep warm. Turn the barbecue up high.

To make the quesadillas, put cheese, coriander, chilli and salt in a bowl and mix well. Sprinkle mixture over one half of each tortilla, then fold the other half over to form a little parcel, pressing the edges together to seal. Brush the grill plate again with oil and cook the quesadillas for 1 minute on each side, or until grill marks appear. Drain on crumpled paper towels; slice in half.

Put a grilled chicken breast on each serving plate with 2 quesadilla halves. Top the chicken with a good dollop of salsa and serve at once.

Serves 4

Sausage and sweet potato wraps

1 tablespoon olive oil
400 g (14 oz) orange sweet potato, peeled and thinly sliced
1 large zucchini (courgette), cut lengthways into 4 pieces
4 thick beef sausages
4 pieces lavash or other flatbread
75 g (2½ oz/⅓ cup) ready-made hummus
175 g (6 oz/1 cup) ready-made tabouleh
sweet chilli sauce, to serve

Heat the grill (broiler) and grill tray to medium. Pour the oil into a bowl and season with salt and pepper. Add the sweet potato and zucchini, gently toss the vegetables to coat, then arrange in a single layer on the preheated grill tray — you will probably need to work in two batches. Grill (broil) vegetables for 5 minutes, then flip them over and cook for another 5 minutes, or until tender. Remove and set aside.

Arrange the sausages on the grill tray and grill for 10–12 minutes, turning once, until browned all over and cooked through. Set aside to cool for 5 minutes, then cut the sausages in half, lengthways.

To assemble, spread each piece of lavash bread with 1 tablespoon hummus and 3 tablespoons tabouleh. Top with the sweet potato, zucchini and the sausage halves, drizzle with sweet chilli sauce, roll up and serve.

Serves 4

Carpetbag burgers with tarragon mayonnaise

Tarragon mayonnaise
2 egg yolks, at room temperature
2 teaspoons dijon mustard
1 tablespoon tarragon vinegar,
  or to taste
200 ml (7 fl oz) olive oil
1 tablespoon finely chopped tarragon

750 g (1 lb 10 oz) minced (ground)
  beef
80 g (2¾ oz/1 cup) fresh white
  breadcrumbs
½ teaspoon finely grated lemon zest
5 drops of Tabasco sauce
1 egg, lightly beaten
6 oysters
olive oil, for brushing
6 good-quality hamburger buns
finely shredded lettuce, to serve

To make tarragon mayonnaise, put the egg yolks, mustard and vinegar in a bowl and whisk well. Whisking constantly, add the oil, a little at a time, making sure it is emulsified before adding more oil. Whisk until thick and creamy. Season with sea salt and freshly ground black pepper, adding a little more vinegar, if needed, then stir in the tarragon.

To make the burgers, put the beef, breadcrumbs, lemon zest, Tabasco and egg in a large bowl and combine well. Divide the mixture into six equal portions. Shape into patties 1.5 cm (⅝ inch) thick. With your thumb, make a cavity in the top of each one. Place an oyster in the cavity and smooth the meat over to enclose it completely. Refrigerate until required.

Heat a frying pan and brush lightly with olive oil. Cook the burgers on medium–high heat for 8 minutes on each side, turning only once.

Meanwhile, split the hamburger buns and lightly toast them, cut side up, under a hot grill (broiler). Keep warm.

Serve burgers on the toasted buns with lettuce and tarragon mayonnaise.

Serves 6

Chicken cacciatore

3 tablespoons olive oil
1 large onion, finely chopped
3 garlic cloves, crushed
1 celery stalk, finely chopped
150 g (5½ oz) pancetta, finely
  chopped
125 g (4½ oz) button mushrooms,
  thinly sliced
4 chicken drumsticks
4 chicken thighs
90 ml (3 fl oz) dry vermouth or dry
  white wine
800 g (1 lb 12 oz) tinned chopped
  tomatoes
¼ teaspoon sugar
1 oregano sprig, plus 4–5 sprigs,
  to garnish
1 rosemary sprig
1 bay leaf

Heat half the oil in a large casserole dish. Add onion, garlic, celery and pancetta. Cook, stirring occasionally, over low heat for 6–8 minutes, or until onion is soft and golden. Add the mushrooms, increase heat and cook, stirring occasionally, for 4 minutes. Spoon onto a plate; set aside.

Add the remaining oil to the dish and lightly brown the chicken pieces, a few at a time. Season them as they brown. Spoon off any excess fat and return all the pieces to the casserole. Add vermouth, increase heat and cook until liquid has almost evaporated.

Stir in the tomatoes, sugar, oregano, rosemary and bay leaf. Add 75 ml (2¼ fl oz) cold water. Bring everything to the boil, then stir in the reserved pancetta mixture. Cover, reduce heat and leave to simmer for 30 minutes, or until the chicken is tender but not falling off the bone. If the liquid is too thin, remove the chicken from the casserole, increase the heat and boil until the sauce has thickened. Discard sprigs of herbs and taste for seasoning. Return the chicken to the dish and add the additional oregano sprigs before serving.

Serves 4

Stifado

4 tablespoons olive oil
1.8 kg (4 lb) round or chuck beef,
   cut into 3 cm (1¼ inch) cubes
1 teaspoon ground cumin
2 onions, finely chopped
3 garlic cloves, crushed
250 ml (9 fl oz/1 cup) dry red wine
3 tablespoons tomato paste
   (concentrated purée)
4 tablespoons red wine vinegar
2 cinnamon sticks
10 cloves
2 bay leaves
2 teaspoons sugar
1 kg (2 lb 4 oz) baby onions
4 tablespoons currants
200 g (7 oz) feta cheese, cut into
   small cubes
steamed rice, to serve

Heat half the oil in a large flameproof casserole dish. Add beef in batches and cook over high heat for 3 minutes, turning to brown all over, and adding more oil as needed. Put the beef in a bowl, then sprinkle with cumin and set aside. Add more oil to the dish, add the onion and garlic and sauté over low heat for 5 minutes, or until onion has softened. Then return the beef to the casserole.

Add wine, increase heat and stir to loosen any bits stuck to the bottom of the dish. Stir in 500 ml (17 fl oz/ 2 cups) water, the tomato paste, vinegar, cinnamon sticks, cloves, bay leaves and sugar. Season with sea salt and freshly ground black pepper and bring to the boil. Reduce the heat to low, cover casserole dish with a double layer of foil, then with the lid. Simmer over low heat for 1 hour.

Peel the onions, cut a small cross into the base, then add to the casserole with the currants. Cook for a further 1 hour, or until the beef is very tender and the sauce is thick. Discard the cinnamon sticks and bay leaves. Stir in the feta and simmer, uncovered, for 3–4 minutes. Serve with steamed rice.

Serves 6–8

Roast chicken with bacon and sage stuffing

2 x 1.2 kg (2 lb 11 oz) chickens
2 tablespoons olive oil
1 small onion, finely chopped
2 slices of bacon, finely chopped, plus
  2 slices of bacon, cut into long strips
1 tablespoon chopped sage
125 g (4½ oz/1½ cups) fresh
  breadcrumbs
1 egg, lightly beaten

Wine gravy
2 tablespoons plain (all-purpose) flour
2 teaspoons worcestershire sauce
2 tablespoons red or white wine
560 ml (19¼ fl oz/2¼ cups) beef or
  chicken stock

Preheat the oven to 180°C (350°F/ Gas 4). Wipe the chickens and pat dry. Heat half the oil in a frying pan (skillet) over medium heat and sauté the onion and chopped bacon for 7–8 minutes, or until the onion is soft and the bacon is starting to brown. Transfer to a bowl, cool, then add sage, breadcrumbs and egg. Mix well and season. Divide the mixture among the chicken cavities. Fold the wings back and tuck them under the chickens. Tie the legs together with string. Place the chickens on a rack in a baking dish, making sure they do not touch, and brush with some of the remaining oil. Pour 250 ml (9 fl oz/ 1 cup) water into the baking dish. Lay the bacon strips across the chicken breasts. Brush the bacon with a little oil. Bake for 45–60 minutes, or until the juices run clear when a thigh is pierced with a skewer. Cover loosely with foil and rest in a warm place.

To make the gravy, discard all but 2 tablespoons of the pan juices. Heat the baking dish over medium heat, stir in the flour and cook, stirring, until well browned. Remove from the heat and gradually add the worcestershire sauce, wine and stock. Return to the heat. Stir until the mixture boils and thickens, then simmer for 2 minutes. Season and serve with the chickens.

Serves 6

Spice-rubbed pork kebabs with garlic sauce

2 teaspoons fennel seeds
2 teaspoons coriander seeds
1 tablespoon olive oil
800 g (1 lb 12 oz) pork neck fillet, trimmed and cut into 2 cm (¾ inch) cubes
lemon wedges, to serve
warm pitta bread, to serve
green salad, to serve (optional)

Garlic sauce
1 thick slice of good-quality, rustic white bread, crusts removed
4 garlic cloves, roughly chopped
½ teaspoon sea salt
3 tablespoons olive oil
1½ tablespoons lemon juice

Toast the fennel and coriander seeds in a dry frying pan over medium–low heat for 30 seconds, or until fragrant, then finely grind them using a spice grinder or mortar and pestle. Tip the spices into a bowl, mix in the olive oil, then add the pork and toss to coat well. Cover and refrigerate for 2 hours.

Meanwhile, to make the garlic sauce, tear the bread into pieces and soak it in a bowl in enough warm water to cover for 5 minutes, then drain well and squeeze dry. Crush the garlic and salt using a mortar and pestle or a small food processor until a smooth paste forms. Add the bread to the garlic mixture, a little at a time, working to a smooth paste. Work in the olive oil 1 tablespoon at a time, then work in 3 tablespoons boiling water, 1 tablespoon at a time. Stir in the lemon juice — the sauce should be thick and smooth.

Preheat a barbecue plate to medium–high. Thread the pork onto metal skewers and season well. Cook the kebabs for 6–8 minutes, or until cooked through, turning onto each side only once. Drizzle with a little garlic sauce and put the remaining sauce in a small bowl to serve at the table. Serve with lemon wedges.

Serves 4

Chilli con carne

1 teaspoon canola or olive oil
1 large onion, chopped
1 green capsicum (pepper) deseeded
and chopped
2 garlic cloves, finely chopped
1 small red chilli, deseeded and
chopped
1–2 teaspoon chilli powder
1 teaspoon ground cumin
500 g (1 lb 2 oz) lean minced (ground)
beef
400 g (14 oz) tin chopped tomatoes
1 tablespoon tomato paste
(concentrated purée)
1 tablespoon polenta
400 g (14 oz/2 cups) basmati rice,
washed and drained
420 g (14½ oz) tin red kidney beans,
drained
1 large handful chopped flat-leaf
(Italian) parsley

Preheat the oven to 180°C (350°F/
Gas 4). Heat the canola or olive oil in
a large casserole dish. Add the onion,
capsicum, garlic and chilli and cook
for 3–4 minutes without browning. Stir
in the chilli powder and cumin and
cook for a further 1 minute.

Increase the heat and add the beef.
Cook for 10–12 minutes, stirring, until
the beef changes colour.

Stir in the tomatoes, tomato paste,
125 ml (4 fl oz/½ cup) water and the
polenta. Cover and place in the oven.
Bake for 40 minutes.

Meanwhile, bring a pan of water to a
boil. Slowly stir in the rice. Bring back
to a boil and cook for 12–15 minutes,
or until tender. Drain.

Stir the kidney beans and parsley into
the meat. Season to taste. Serve hot
with the rice and a salad.

Serves 4

Chicken tamales

Dough
100 g (3½ oz) butter, softened
1 garlic clove, crushed
1 teaspoon ground cumin
210 g (7½ oz/1½ cups) masa harina
   (see Tip)
4 tablespoons pouring cream
4 tablespoons chicken stock

1 corn cob
2 tablespoons oil
150 g (5½ oz) boneless, skinless
   chicken breast
2 garlic cloves, crushed
1 red chilli, seeded and chopped
1 red onion, chopped
1 red capsicum (pepper), chopped
2 tomatoes, peeled and chopped
sour cream, to serve
chopped coriander (cilantro) leaves,
   to serve

To make the dough, beat the butter with electric beaters until creamy. Add garlic, cumin and 1 teaspoon salt and mix well. Add the masa harina and the cream and stock alternately, beating until combined.

Cook the corn in boiling water for 6 minutes, or until tender. Cool, then cut off the kernels. Heat oil in a frying pan, cook the chicken for 5 minutes each side, until golden. Remove, cool and shred finely. Add garlic, chilli and onion to pan and cook for 3 minutes, or until soft. Stir in the capsicum and corn and cook for 3 minutes. Add the chicken, tomato and 1 teaspoon salt. Simmer for 15 minutes, or until liquid is reduced.

Cut 12 pieces of baking paper into 20 x 15 cm (8 x 6 inch) pieces. Spread a thick layer of dough over each piece, leaving a border at each end. Spoon filling in the centre, roll up and secure with string. Arrange in a large steamer in a single layer. Cover and steam over a large saucepan of boiling water for 35 minutes, or until firm. Arrange three tamales on each plate and serve with sour cream and coriander.

Serves 4

Tip: Masa harina is a type of cornflour (cornstarch) and is available in larger supermarkets and health-food stores.

Braised oxtail

3 tablespoons extra virgin olive oil
16 small oxtail pieces, about 1.5 kg
  (3 lb 5 oz) in total
4 baby potatoes, cut in half
1 large onion, chopped
2 carrots, chopped
250 g (9 oz) button mushrooms
2 tablespoons plain (all-purpose) flour
750 ml (26 fl oz/3 cups) beef stock
1 teaspoon dried marjoram
2 tablespoons worcestershire sauce

Preheat the oven to 180°C (350°F/
Gas 4). Heat 2 tablespoons of the
olive oil in a large, heavy-based frying
pan. Add oxtail in batches and cook
over medium–high heat for 5 minutes,
turning to brown all over. Transfer to a
deep casserole dish. Add potatoes.

Heat remaining oil in the pan. Add
the onion and carrot and sauté over
medium heat for 5 minutes, or until
the onion has softened. Transfer to
the casserole dish.

Add the mushrooms to the frying pan,
adding a little more oil, if needed, and
sauté over medium heat for 5 minutes.
Stir in flour, reduce heat to low and stir
for about 2 minutes. Season with sea
salt and freshly ground black pepper,
then gradually add the stock, stirring
until the liquid boils and thickens. Stir
in the marjoram and worcestershire
sauce, then pour the mixture over the
ingredients in the casserole dish.

Bake, covered, for 1½ hours. Remove
the lid, stir well and cook, uncovered,
for a further 30 minutes, or until the
meat is very tender.

Serves 6

Beef rolls in tomato sauce

Tomato sauce
oil spray
1 onion, finely chopped
1 celery stalk, finely chopped
124 ml (4 fl oz/½ cup) red wine
2 x 400 g (14 oz) tins chopped
  tomatoes
2 tablespoons tomato paste
  (concentrated puree)
2 teaspoons sugar
2 sprigs thyme

Parsley stuffing
1 large handful flat-leaf (Italian)
  parsley, chopped
45 g (1½ oz/½ cup) grated parmesan
3 garlic cloves, finely chopped
zest of 2 large lemons

8 x 85 g (3 oz) minute steaks
chopped herbs, to serve

Heat a heavy-based frying pan (skillet) that is 8 cm (3 inch) deep and 24 cm (9½ inch) in diameter (across the base) and spray with the oil. Cook the onion and celery for 2–3 minutes, or until softened. Add the wine and cook until reduced by two-thirds. Add the tomatoes, tomato paste, sugar and thyme sprigs. Add 500 ml (17 fl oz/2 cups) water, simmer, stirring occasionally, for 30 minutes, or until thickened and reduced. Remove the thyme sprigs.

Meanwhile, combine the parsley, cheese, garlic and lemon zest. Flatten the steaks with a meat mallet to an even 5 mm (¼ inch) thick. Pat dry with paper towels. Divide the stuffing evenly over the steaks. Roll up firmly and secure each with a toothpick. Spray a large, non-stick frying pan with oil. Brown the beef rolls all over, then transfer to the tomato sauce. Arrange in a single layer. Bring to the boil, then lower the heat, cover and simmer for 45 minutes, or until tender. Turn once or twice during cooking.

Serve two beef rolls per person and spoon over the sauce. Top with the chopped herbs.

Serves 4

Pork chops with braised red cabbage

Braised red cabbage
2 tablespoons clarified butter
1 onion, finely chopped
1 garlic clove, crushed
1 small red cabbage, shredded
1 apple, peeled, cored and finely
  sliced
4 tablespoons red wine
1 tablespoon red wine vinegar
1/4 teaspoon ground cloves
1 tablespoon finely chopped sage

1 tablespoon clarified butter
4 x 175 g (6 oz) pork chops,
  trimmed
4 tablespoons white wine
420 ml (14 1/2 fl oz/1 2/3 cups)
  chicken stock
3 tablespoons thick (double/heavy)
  cream
1 1/2 tablespoons dijon mustard
4 sage leaves

To make the braised cabbage, heat butter in a large saucepan, add onion and garlic and sauté over medium heat for 6–7 minutes, or until the onion has softened. Add remaining ingredients and season with salt and freshly ground black pepper. Cover and cook for 30 minutes over very low heat. Remove the lid and stir over medium–high heat for 5 minutes so that liquid evaporates.

Meanwhile, prepare the pork. Heat the butter in a frying pan, add pork and brown over medium–high heat for 2 minutes on each side. Season with sea salt and freshly ground black pepper. Pour in wine and stock, then cover and simmer for 15–20 minutes, or until tender. Remove the pork to a warmed plate, cover loosely with foil and leave to rest.

Strain the liquid from the frying pan, then return it to the frying pan. Bring to the boil and cook until reduced by two-thirds. Add the cream and mustard and stir over very low heat until the sauce has thickened slightly; do not allow the cream to boil.

Place the pork on warmed serving plates, drizzle generously with the sauce and garnish with a sage leaf. Serve with the braised red cabbage.

Serves 4

Cajun chicken with fresh tomato and corn

2 corn cobs
2 vine-ripened tomatoes, diced
1 Lebanese (short) cucumber, diced
2 tablespoons roughly chopped
  coriander (cilantro) leaves
4 boneless, skinless chicken breast
  (about 200 g/7 oz each)
3 tablespoons cajun seasoning
2 tablespoons lime juice
lime wedges, to serve

Cook the corn cobs in a saucepan of boiling water for 5 minutes, or until tender. Remove the kernels using a sharp knife and place in a bowl with the tomato, cucumber and coriander. Season and mix well.

Heat a chargrill pan or barbecue plate to medium heat and brush lightly with oil. Pound each chicken breast between two sheets of plastic wrap with a mallet or rolling pin until 2 cm (1/4 inch) thick. Lightly coat the chicken with the cajun seasoning and shake off any excess. Cook for 5 minutes on each side, or until cooked through.

Just before serving, stir the lime juice into the salsa. Place a chicken breast on each plate and spoon the salsa on the side. Serve with the lime wedges, a green salad and crusty bread.

Serves 4

Stir-fried Thai beef

14 oz (400 g) lean sirloin steak, trimmed
2–3 birds-eye chillies, deseeded and finely chopped
3 garlic cloves, crushed
1 teaspoon soft brown sugar
2 tablespoons fish sauce
2 teaspoons canola oil
400 g (14 oz/2 cups) jasmine rice
150 g (5½ oz) yard-long beans, sliced into 3 cm (1¼ inch) lengths
150 g (5½ oz) sugar snap peas, trimmed
1 large carrot, thinly sliced
1 large handful Thai basil
1–2 birds-eye chillies, deseeded and finely sliced (optional)

Slice the meat as thinly as possible, across the grain. Put in a non-metallic bowl with chilli, garlic, brown sugar, fish sauce and 1 teaspoon oil. Toss well to combine, cover and refrigerate for 2 hours.

Half an hour before serving, wash the rice well in a sieve until the water runs clear. Put rice in a large saucepan with 750 ml (26 fl oz/3 cups) water, bring to the boil and boil for 1 minute. Cover, reduce heat as low as possible and cook for 10 minutes. Turn off the heat and leave saucepan covered for 10 minutes. Fluff the rice with a fork.

Blanch the beans, sugar snap peas and carrot in a large saucepan of boiling water for 2 minutes, drain and refresh. Heat remaining oil in a large, non-stick wok until very hot and stir-fry the beef in two batches over high heat until just browned.

Return all beef to the wok with the blanched vegetables and the basil. Stir-fry for 1–2 minutes, or until warmed through. Garnish with sliced chillies, if using, and serve with rice.

Serves 4

Chicken provençale

1 tablespoon olive oil
1.5 kg (3 lb 5 oz) chicken pieces
1 onion, chopped
1 red capsicum (pepper), chopped
4 tablespoons dry white wine
4 tablespoons chicken stock
425 g (15 oz) tinned chopped
    tomatoes
2 tablespoons tomato paste
    (concentrated purée)
90 g (3¼ oz/½ cup) black olives
small handful basil, shredded

Heat oil in a saucepan over high heat, add chicken, in batches, and cook for 3–4 minutes, or until browned. Return all the chicken to the pan and add the onion and capsicum. Cook 3 minutes, or until the onion is soft.

Add the wine, stock, tomato, tomato paste and olives, and bring to the boil. Reduce the heat, cover and simmer for 30 minutes. Remove the lid, turn the chicken pieces over and cook for another 30 minutes, or until the chicken is tender and the sauce thickened. Season to taste, sprinkle with the basil and serve with rice.

Serves 6

亦反映政府……………位，未有受到挑戰而脚

震。有料老友話，唐廚的説話其實亦暗藏機鋒。

今時今日，陳太坐在議員席上，發言質問政府，

Beef and spinach curry

2 tablespoons oil
1 onion, finely chopped
2 garlic cloves, finely chopped
2 teaspoons ground cumin
2 teaspoons ground coriander
2 teaspoons paprika
1 teaspoon garam masala
1 teaspoon turmeric
½ teaspoon finely chopped red chilli
1 teaspoon finely chopped green chilli
2 teaspoons grated fresh ginger
500 g (1 lb 2 oz) lean minced (ground)
  beef or lamb
1 tomato, chopped
250 ml (9 fl oz/1 cup) beef stock
  or water
500 g (1 lb 2 oz) English spinach,
  chopped
200 g (7 oz) plain yoghurt

Heat 1 tablespoon of oil in a large saucepan and cook the onion over a medium heat until golden brown. Add garlic, cumin, coriander, paprika, garam masala, turmeric, red and green chilli and the grated ginger and stir for 1 minute. Remove; set aside.

Heat remaining oil in the pan and brown meat over high heat, breaking up any lumps with a fork or wooden spoon. Return onion mixture to pan and add tomato and stock or water.

Bring the mixture to the boil and then reduce the heat and simmer for about 1 hour. Season with salt, to taste. Meanwhile, cook the spinach briefly. Just before serving, add the spinach to the mixture and stir in the yoghurt.

Serves 4

Note: If possible, make the meat mixture in advance and refrigerate overnight for the flavours to develop.

Fish

Caribbean fish soup

2 tomatoes
2 tablespoons oil
4 French shallots, finely chopped
2 celery stalks, chopped
1 large red capsicum (pepper),
    chopped
1 Scotch bonnet chilli, deseeded and
    finely chopped (see Note)
½ teaspoon ground allspice
½ teaspoon freshly grated nutmeg
850 ml (30 fl oz) fish stock
275 g (9¾ oz) orange sweet potato,
    peeled and cut into cubes
60 ml (2 fl oz/¼ cup) lime juice
500 g (1 lb 2 oz) skinless sea bream,
    sea bass or cod fillets, cut into
    chunks

Score a cross in the base of each tomato. Soak tomatoes in boiling water for 30 seconds, then plunge them into cold water. Drain and peel the skin away from the cross. Chop the tomatoes, discarding the cores, and reserving any juices.

Heat the oil in a large saucepan, then add the shallots, celery, capsicum, chilli, allspice and nutmeg. Cook for 4–5 minutes, or until the vegetables have softened, stirring now and then. Tip in the chopped tomatoes (including their juices) and stock and bring to the boil. Reduce heat to medium and add sweet potato. Season to taste with salt and pepper and cook for about 15 minutes, or until the sweet potato is tender.

Add the lime juice and chunks of fish to the saucepan and poach gently for 4–5 minutes, or until the fish is cooked through. Season to taste, then serve with lots of crusty bread.

Serves 6

Note: Scotch bonnet chillies resemble a mini capsicums (bell peppers) and can be green, red or orange. They are extremely hot but have a good, slightly acidic flavour.

Fish patties

2 tablespoons canola oil
500 g (1 lb 2 oz) boneless white fish
fillets
1 leek, halved lengthways, washed
and chopped
2 garlic cloves, crushed
700 g (1 lb 9 oz) white-skinned
potatoes, peeled and quartered
30 g (1 oz/¼ cup) chopped spring
onions (scallions)
sea salt flakes
iceberg lettuce leaves, to serve
fruit chutney, to serve

Heat 2 teaspoons of the oil in a large
non-stick frying pan over medium
heat. Add the fish fillets and cook for
3 minutes each side, or until cooked.
Set aside to cool.

Flake the fish with a fork. Heat another
2 teaspoons of oil in the same pan
over medium heat. Cook the leek and
garlic, stirring often, for 5–6 minutes,
or until the leek softens. Set aside on
a plate. Wipe pan with paper towels.

Meanwhile, put the potatoes in a large
saucepan. Cover with cold water and
bring to the boil. Boil for 15 minutes,
or until the potatoes are tender. Drain
well. Mash with a potato masher.

Combine the mashed potato, flaked
fish, leek mixture and spring onions
in a large bowl and mix thoroughly.
Season with a little salt. Shape into
eight patties. Put on a plate, cover
and refrigerate for 1 hour.

Heat the remaining oil in the frying pan
over medium heat. Cook patties for
3–4 minutes on each side, or until light
golden and heated through. Serve
with lettuce and chutney.

Serves 4

Tuscan bread salad

200 g (7 oz) ciabatta bread
8 vine-ripened tomatoes
4 tablespoons olive oil
1 tablespoon lemon juice
1½ tablespoons red wine vinegar
6 anchovy fillets, finely chopped
1 tablespoon baby capers, rinsed,
    squeezed dry and finely chopped
1 garlic clove, crushed
3 handfuls basil

Preheat the oven to 220°C (425°F/ Gas 7). Tear bread into 2 cm (¾ inch) pieces, spread on a baking tray and bake for 5–7 minutes, or until golden on the outside. Leave toasted bread on a wire rack to cool.

Score a cross in the base of each tomato. Place tomatoes in a heatproof bowl and cover with boiling water. Leave for 20 seconds, then plunge them into cold water and peel the skin away from the cross. Cut four of the tomatoes in half and squeeze the juice and seeds into a bowl, reserving and chopping the flesh. Add the oil, lemon juice, vinegar, anchovies, capers and garlic to the tomato juice, and season.

Seed and slice remaining tomatoes, and place in a bowl with the reserved tomato and most of the basil. Add dressing and toasted bread; toss to combine. Garnish with remaining basil; season. Leave for at least 15 minutes. Serve at room temperature.

Serves 6

Fish pie

Potato topping
500 g (1 lb 2 oz) floury potatoes
   (such as Idaho, King Edward), diced
60 ml (2 fl oz/¼ cup) milk or cream
1 egg, lightly beaten
30 g (1 oz) butter
60 g (2¼ oz) cheddar cheese, finely
   grated

800 g (1 lb 12 oz) skinless ling,
   snapper, cod or haddock fillets,
   cut into large chunks
375 ml (13 fl oz/1½ cups) milk
30 g (1 oz) butter
1 onion, finely chopped
1 garlic clove, crushed
2 tablespoons plain (all-purpose) flour
2 tablespoons lemon juice
2 teaspoons lemon zest
1 tablespoon chopped dill

Preheat the oven to 180°C (350°F/
Gas 4). To make the topping, steam
the potatoes until tender. Mash, then
push to one side of the pan, add the
milk and heat gently. Beat the milk
into the potato until it is fluffy, then
season and stir in the egg and butter.
Mix in half the cheddar, then set aside
and keep warm.

Put the fish in a frying pan and cover
with milk. Bring to the boil, reduce
the heat and simmer for 2 minutes, or
until fish is opaque and flaky. Drain,
reserving the milk, and put the fish in
a 1.5 litre (6 cup) ovenproof dish.

Melt the butter in a saucepan and
cook onion and garlic for 2 minutes.
Stir in the flour and cook for 1 minute,
or until pale and foaming. Remove
from the heat and gradually stir in
the reserved milk. Return to the heat
and stir constantly until it boils and
thickens. Reduce the heat and simmer
for 2 minutes. Add the lemon juice,
zest and dill, and season. Mix with the
fish. Spoon the topping over the fish
and top with the remaining cheddar.
Bake for 35 minutes, or until golden.

Serves 4

Grilled sardines with basil and lemon

1 lemon
12 whole sardines, cleaned and
  scaled
coarse sea salt, for seasoning
4 tablespoons olive oil
3 tablespoons torn basil leaves
  or small whole leaves

Preheat the grill (broiler) to very hot.

Thinly slice the lemon, then cut each slice in half. Insert several pieces in each sardine. Season both sides of each fish with the sea salt and some freshly ground black pepper.

Put the sardines on a baking tray, drizzle with half the olive oil and grill (broil) for 3 minutes on each side, or until just cooked through; the flesh inside the sardines should be opaque. Remove and place in a shallow dish.

Scatter the basil over the sardines and drizzle with the remaining olive oil. Serve warm or at room temperature.

Serves 4

Variation: Small herring or mackerel can be used instead of sardines.

Salmon kedgeree

1 litre (35 fl oz/4 cups) fish stock
400 g (14 oz) salmon fillet
3 tablespoons butter
2 tablespoons oil
1 onion, chopped
2 teaspoons madras curry paste
200 g (7 oz/1 cup) long-grain rice
2 hard-boiled eggs, cut into wedges
3 tablespoons chopped parsley
3 tablespoons cream
lemon wedges, to serve

Pour stock in a frying pan and bring to the boil. Add salmon, cover, then reduce the heat to a simmer. Cook for 3 minutes, or until fish becomes firm when pressed and turns opaque. Lift out the salmon and flake it into large pieces by gently pulling it apart with your hands.

Melt half of the butter in a frying pan with the oil, add the onion and cook over a low heat until the onion softens and turns translucent. Stir in the curry paste, then add the rice and mix well until the rice is coated. Add the fish stock, mix well, then bring the mixture to the boil.

Simmer rice, covered, over a very low heat for 8 minutes. Add salmon and cook, covered, for another 5 minutes, until all the liquid is absorbed. If the rice is too dry and not cooked, add a splash of boiling water and keep cooking for a further 1–2 minutes.

Stir in the rest of the butter, the eggs, parsley and cream (you can leave out the cream if you prefer—the result won't be so rich). Serve kedgeree with the lemon wedges to squeeze over.

Serves 4

Herbed fish tartlets

150 g (5½ oz/1¼ cups) plain
  (all-purpose) flour
90 g (3¼ oz) butter, chopped
1 tablespoon chopped thyme
1 tablespoon chopped dill
2 tablespoons chopped flat-leaf
  (Italian) parsley
90 g (3¼ oz) cheddar cheese, finely
  grated
60–80 ml (2–2½ fl oz/¼–⅓ cup)
  iced water

Filling
400 g (14 oz) skinless firm white
  fish fillets
2 spring onions (scallions), finely
  chopped
2 tablespoons chopped parsley
60 g (2¼ oz) cheddar cheese, finely
  grated
2 eggs
125 ml (4 fl oz/½ cup) pouring cream

Grease eight 10 cm (4 inch) fluted flan (tart) tins. Sift the flour into a bowl. Using your fingertips, rub in the butter until the mixture resembles breadcrumbs. Stir in the herbs and cheese. Make a well in the centre. Add almost all the water and mix with a flat-bladed knife, using a cutting action, until mixture comes together in beads. Add more water if needed. Gather into a ball, wrap in plastic wrap and refrigerate for 15 minutes. Preheat the oven to 210°C (415°F/Gas 6–7). Divide the pastry into eight and roll out to fit the tins. Ease into the tins, trim the edges and place on a baking tray. Cover each tin with baking paper and spread with baking beads or uncooked rice. Bake for 10 minutes, remove the paper and beads and bake for another 10 minutes, or until lightly browned. Cool.

To make the filling, put the fish in a frying pan and cover with cold water. Bring to the boil, reduce the heat and simmer for 3 minutes. Remove with a slotted spoon and drain on paper towels. Cool, then flake with a fork. Divide among cases and sprinkle with spring onion, parsley and cheddar. Whisk eggs and cream and pour over fish. Bake for 25 minutes, or until set and golden brown.

Makes 8

Fish cutlets with ginger and chilli

4 x 175 g (6 oz) firm white fish cutlets, such as snapper or blue-eye
5 cm (2 inch) piece of ginger, shredded
2 garlic cloves, chopped
4 red chillies, seeded and chopped
2 tablespoons chopped coriander (cilantro) stems
3 spring onions (scallions), cut into short, fine shreds
2 tablespoons lime juice

Line a steamer with banana leaves or baking paper and punch with holes. Place fish in the steamer, top with the ginger, garlic, chilli and coriander and cover with a lid. Sit steamer over a wok or saucepan of boiling water and steam for about 8 minutes, or until the fish flakes easily.

Sprinkle the spring onion and lime juice over the fish, cover and steam for an extra 30 seconds. Serve with steamed jasmine rice.

Serves 4

Battered fish and chunky wedges

3 all-purpose potatoes
oil, for deep-frying
150 g (5 oz/1 cup) self-raising flour
1 egg, beaten
185 ml (6 fl oz/³⁄₄ cup) beer (fizzy or
  flat)
4 white fish fillets
plain (all-purpose) flour, for dusting
125 g (4¹⁄₂ oz/¹⁄₂ cup) ready-made
  tartare sauce

Wash the potatoes. Cut into thick wedges, leaving the skin on, then dry with paper towels. Fill a large heavy-based saucepan two-thirds full with oil and heat. Gently lower the potato wedges into medium–hot oil. Cook for 4 minutes, or until tender and lightly browned. Carefully remove wedges from the oil with a slotted spoon and drain on paper towels.

Sift the self-raising flour with some freshly ground black pepper into a bowl. Make a well in the centre and add the egg and beer. Stir until just combined and smooth. Dust fish in the plain flour, shaking off the excess. Add fillets one at a time to the batter and toss until well coated. Remove from the batter, draining off excess. Working with one piece of fish at a time, gently lower it into medium–hot oil. Cook for 2 minutes, or until it is golden, crisp and cooked through. Carefully remove with a slotted spoon; drain on paper towels. Keep warm.

Return the wedges to the medium-hot oil. Cook for another 2 minutes, or until golden brown and crisp. Remove with a slotted spoon; drain on paper towels. Serve the wedges immediately with the fish and tartare sauce.

Serves 4

African fish pie

25 g (1 oz) butter, plus a little extra,
  for greasing the tin
2 onions, finely chopped
2 garlic cloves, crushed
2 tablespoons mild curry powder
½ teaspoon turmeric
grated zest and juice of 1 small lemon
100 g (3½ oz) raisins
50 g (¾ oz/⅓ cup) whole blanched
  almonds, chopped
250 ml (9 fl oz/1 cup) milk
40 g (approximately 2 thick slices)
  white bread
1 kg (2 lb 4 oz) skinless snook, pike or
  cod fillet, finely chopped
2 large eggs

Preheat the oven to 190°C (375°F/
Gas 5). Heat the butter in a frying pan
(skillet) and add the onion. Cook for
7–8 minutes, or until soft and lightly
golden, stirring occasionally.

Add the garlic and cook for a further
2 minutes. Mix in 1 tablespoon of the
curry powder, the turmeric, lemon
zest and juice, raisins and almonds.
Remove from the heat and allow to
cool for 10 minutes.

Pour 2½ tablespoons of the milk into
a bowl and soak the bread in it for
10 minutes, turning after 5 minutes.
Squeeze the bread dry, then tear into
small pieces and put in a bowl. Add
the fish, one egg and the mixture from
the frying pan to the bowl, season
well and combine. Scoop into a lightly
buttered non-stick 23 cm (9 inch)
square tin 7 cm (2¾ inches) high.
Bake 15 minutes. Towards the end of
the cooking time, whisk together the
remaining milk, curry powder and egg.
Pour liquid over the top of the mixture
in tin. Bake for a further 45 minutes,
or until set. Cool 15 minutes, then cut
into squares to serve.

Serves 6

Fish fillets with fennel and red capsicum salsa

750 g (1 lb 10 oz) small new potatoes
1 teaspoon fennel seeds
125 ml (4 fl oz/½ cup) olive oil
2 tablespoons, rinsed and squeezed
  dry, baby capers
1 small red capsicum (pepper),
  deseeded and finely diced
250 g (9 oz) mixed salad leaves,
  washed
2 tablespoons balsamic vinegar
4 white fish fillets (blue-eye cod or
  John Dory), about 200 g/7 oz each

Cook the potatoes in a saucepan of boiling water for 15–20 minutes, or until tender. Drain and keep warm.

Meanwhile, to make the salsa, dry-fry the fennel seeds in a frying pan over medium heat for 1 minute, or until fragrant. Remove the seeds and heat 1 tablespoon oil in the same pan over medium heat. When the oil is hot but not smoking, flash-fry the capers for 1–2 minutes, or until crisp. Remove from the pan. Heat 1 tablespoon oil and cook the capsicum, stirring for 4–5 minutes, or until cooked through. Remove and combine with the fennel seeds and fried capers.

Place the salad leaves in a serving bowl. To make dressing, combine the balsamic vinegar and 3 tablespoons olive oil in a bowl. Add 1 tablespoon to the salsa, then toss the rest through the salad leaves.

Wipe the frying pan, then heat the remaining oil over medium–high heat. Season the fish well. When the oil is hot, but not smoking, cook the fish for 2–3 minutes each side, or until cooked through. Serve immediately with the salsa, potatoes and salad.

Serves 4

Jansson's temptation

15 anchovy fillets
80 ml (2½ fl oz/⅓ cup) milk
60 g (2¼ oz) butter
2 large onions, thinly sliced
5 potatoes, peeled, cut into
   5 mm (¼ inch) slices, then thinly
   sliced
500 g (2 cups) thick (double/heavy)
   cream

Preheat the oven to 200°C (400°F/ Gas 6). Soak the anchovies in the milk for 5 minutes to reduce their saltiness. Drain and rinse.

Melt half the butter in a frying pan and cook the onion over medium heat for 5 minutes, or until golden and tender. Chop the remaining butter into small cubes and set aside.

Spread half the potato over the base of a shallow ovenproof dish, top with the anchovies and onion and finish with the remaining potato.

Pour half the cream over the potato and scatter the butter cubes on top. Bake for 20 minutes, or until golden. Pour the remaining cream over the top and cook for another 40 minutes, or until the potato feels tender when the point of a knife is inserted. Season with salt and pepper before serving.

Serves 4

Crispy fish and lentils

4 tablespoons plain (all-purpose) flour
4 (600 g/1 lb 5 oz) boneless white fish
  fillets
2 tablespoons oil
4 spring onions (scallions), diagonally
  sliced
2 garlic cloves, crushed
2 x 400 g (14 oz) tins brown lentils,
  rinsed and drained
250 g (9 oz) green beans, trimmed

Combine the flour and a little salt on a plate. Coat fish fillets in seasoned flour, shaking off any excess. Heat 1 tablespoon of oil in a large non-stick frying pan over medium–high heat. Add the fish and cook for 3–4 minutes on each side, or until cooked through and lightly browned, depending on the size of your frying pan you may need to cook the fish in batches.

Meanwhile, heat remaining oil in a large saucepan. Cook spring onion and garlic for 2 minutes, or until softened. Add the lentils. Toss for a few minutes, or until lentils are heated through.

Steam or microwave the beans for a few minutes, or until tender.

Serve the fish with warm lentils and the green beans.

Serves 4

Moroccan stuffed sardines

Couscous stuffing
75 g (2½ oz) couscous
2 tablespoons olive oil
2 tablespoons finely chopped dried
    apricots
3 tablespoons raisins
1 tablespoon flaked toasted almonds
1 tablespoon chopped parsley
1 tablespoon chopped mint
grated zest of 1 orange

2 tablespoons orange juice
1 teaspoon finely chopped preserved
    lemon rind
1 teaspoon ground cinnamon
½ teaspoon harissa
16 large fresh or preserved vine leaves
16 large fresh sardines, butterflied
oil, for brushing
lemon wedges, to serve
400 g (14 oz) thick plain yoghurt

Start by making the couscous stuffing. Put couscous in a bowl and add half the oil and 50 ml (1¾ fl oz) of boiling water. Stir and leave for 10 minutes to allow the couscous to absorb the liquid. Fluff up the couscous grains with a fork and add the remaining oil and stuffing ingredients. Season to taste and mix well.

Preheat a barbecue flat plate to medium. If you are using fresh vine leaves, bring a saucepan of water to the boil and blanch the leaves in batches for 30 seconds, then remove and pat dry on paper towels. If you are using preserved vine leaves, simply rinse and pat them dry.

Divide couscous stuffing between the sardines, saving any leftover couscous for serving time. Fold the sardine fillets back together to enclose the stuffing. Gently wrap a vine leaf around each sardine and secure with a toothpick.

Lightly brush hotplate with oil and cook sardines for 6 minutes, turning halfway through the cooking. Serve hot with lemon wedges, a dollop of yoghurt and any remaining couscous.

Serves 4 as a starter

Fish provençale

1 small red capsicum (pepper), thinly
  sliced
250 g (9 oz/1 cup) bottled pasta
  sauce
1 tablespoon chopped thyme
40 g (1½ oz) butter
4 large skinless perch or snapper
  fillets
thyme sprigs, for garnish

Combine capsicum, pasta sauce and
chopped thyme in a bowl.

Melt half the butter in a large non-stick
frying pan over a high heat and cook
the fish for 1 minute, adding remaining
butter as you go. Turn the fish over
and pour on the capsicum mixture.
Simmer for 10 minutes, or until the
fish is cooked. Season to taste and
garnish with thyme sprigs. Serve with
roasted potato slices and crusty bread
to soak up the juices.

Serves 4

Salmon fillet with bean purée

4 x 175 g (6 oz) salmon fillets
2 teaspoons canola oil
1 garlic clove, crushed
2 tablespoons white wine vinegar
1 teaspoon finely grated lime zest
2 tablespoons chopped dill
600 g (1 lb 5 oz) tin cannellini (white)
  beans, rinsed and drained
1 bay leaf
250 ml (9 fl oz/1 cup) chicken stock
500 g (1 lb 2 oz/1 bunch) baby English
  spinach leaves, roughly chopped

Place the salmon in a non-metallic dish. Combine oil, garlic, vinegar, lime zest and dill, pour over the fish, cover and leave to stand for 10 minutes.

Place the beans, bay leaf and stock in a saucepan. Simmer for 10 minutes. Remove the bay leaf. Place in a food processor and purée. Season with salt and freshly ground black pepper.

Drain salmon, reserving the marinade. Cook in a non-stick frying pan over a high heat for 4 minutes on each side, or until crisp and golden. Remove, add marinade to the pan and boil.

Steam the spinach until wilted. Serve the salmon fillets on the purée and spinach and drizzle over the marinade. Serve with brown bread.

Serves 4

Mexican baked fish

3 tomatoes, chopped
1/2 teaspoon ground cumin
1/2 teaspoon ground allspice
1/2 teaspoon ground cinnamon
1 habanero chilli, deseeded and
  finely chopped
4 tablespoons coriander (cilantro)
  leaves
4 x 175–200 g (6–7 oz) skinless red
  snapper, flake, grouper or cod fillets
1/2 small red onion, chopped
1/2 small green capsicum (pepper),
  chopped
1 tablespoon sour or Seville orange
  juice, or 2 teaspoons orange juice
  and 2 teaspoons vinegar
juice of 1 lime

Preheat the oven to 190°C (375°F/
Gas 5). Mix the tomatoes in a bowl
with the cumin, allspice, cinnamon,
chilli and coriander.

Cut four squares of foil, each large
enough to enclose a fish fillet. Place
a piece of fish on each of the foil
squares and divide tomato mixture
among the four fillets.

Combine the red onion and green
capsicum and divide among the
parcels. Stir the orange and lime juice
together and drizzle over the top of
the fish and vegetables. Season with
salt and pepper.

Wrap the fish in the foil and transfer
the parcels to a baking dish. Bake for
15–20 minutes, or until the fish flakes
easily when tested with a fork.

Serves 4

Thai ginger fish with coriander butter

60 g (2¼ oz) butter, at room
    temperature
1 tablespoon finely chopped coriander
    (cilantro) leaves
2 tablespoons lime juice
1 tablespoon vegetable oil
1 tablespoon grated palm sugar or
    soft brown sugar
4 long red chillies, deseeded and
    chopped
2 lemongrass stems, trimmed and
    halved
4 x 200 g (7 oz) firm white fish fillets
    (such as blue-eye or john dory)
1 lime, finely sliced
1 tablespoon finely shredded fresh
    ginger

Thoroughly combine the butter and coriander and roll into a log. Wrap in plastic wrap and chill in the refrigerator for at least 30 minutes, or until you are ready to serve.

Combine the lime juice, oil, sugar and chilli in a small non-metallic bowl and stir until the sugar has dissolved.

Lay a piece of lemongrass in the centre of a sheet of foil large enough to fully enclose one fish fillet. Place a fish fillet on top and brush surface with the lime juice mixture. Top with some lime slices and ginger shreds, then wrap up into a secure parcel. Repeat with remaining ingredients to make four parcels.

Line a large steamer with baking paper and punch paper with holes. Lay fish parcels on top in a single layer and cover with a lid. Sit steamer over a wok or pan of boiling water and steam for 8–10 minutes, or until fish flakes easily when tested with a fork.

Place parcels on individual plates and serve them open with slices of coriander butter and some steamed rice and green vegetables.

Serves 4

Vegetarian

Green lentil and vegetable curry

1 teaspoon canola oil
1 large onion, chopped
2 garlic cloves, chopped
1–2 tablespoons curry paste
1 teaspoon ground turmeric
200 g (7 oz/1 cup) green lentils, rinsed
    and drained
1.25 litres (44 fl oz/5 cups) vegetable
    stock or water
1 large carrot, cut into 2 cm (3/4 inch)
    cubes
2 potatoes, cut into 2 cm (3/4 inch)
    cubes
250 g (9 oz) sweet potato, peeled and
    cut into 2 cm (3/4 inch) cubes
350 g (12 oz) cauliflower, broken into
    small florets
150 g (5½ oz) green beans, trimmed
    and halved
basil, to serve
coriander (cilantro) leaves, to serve

Heat oil in a saucepan over a medium heat. Add the onion and garlic, and cook for 3 minutes, or until softened. Stir in the curry paste and turmeric and stir for 1 minute. Add the lentils and stock or water.

Bring to a boil, then reduce the heat. Cover and simmer for 30 minutes, then add the carrot, potatoes and sweet potato. Simmer, covered, for 20 minutes, or until the lentils and vegetables are tender.

Add the cauliflower and beans once most of the liquid has been absorbed. Remove lid and simmer for a further few minutes if there is too much liquid.

Serve hot with brown or basmati rice and top with basil and coriander.

Serves 4

Summer salad with marinated tofu steaks

500 g (1 lb 2 oz) block firm tofu
2 tablespoons balsamic vinegar
1 tablespoon olive oil
1 garlic clove, crushed

Summer salad
250 g (9 oz/1 punnet) cherry
  tomatoes, halved
1/2 red onion, thinly sliced
1 small Lebanese (short) cucumber,
  sliced
1 handful basil leaves, shredded
12 pitted kalamata olives, halved
2 teaspoons balsamic vinegar
2 teaspoons extra virgin olive oil

Cut tofu horizontally into four thin steaks, or four large cubes, if you prefer. Place in a large, shallow non-metallic dish and drizzle with the vinegar and oil. Add garlic and season well with salt and pepper. Use your fingers to rub mixture evenly all over the tofu. Cover; refrigerate for at least 30 minutes, or up to 4 hours, turning tofu occasionally.

Preheat a barbecue flat plate to moderately hot. When you're nearly ready to eat, make the salad. Put the tomato, onion, cucumber, basil, olives and vinegar in a bowl, drizzle with the oil, toss together gently. Season well.

Cook tofu on hotplate for 2 minutes on each side, or until golden. Transfer to four serving plates and pile salad over the top. Serve at once, with crusty bread.

Serves 4

Oven-baked potato, leek and olives

2 tablespoons extra virgin olive oil
1 leek, finely sliced
375 ml (13 fl oz/1½ cups) vegetable
  stock
2 teaspoons chopped thyme
1 kg (2 lb 4 oz) potatoes, unpeeled,
  cut into thin slices
6–8 pitted black olives, sliced
60 g (2¼ oz/½ cup) grated parmesan
  cheese
30 g (1 oz) butter, chopped

Preheat the oven to 180°C (350°F/ Gas 4). Brush a shallow 1.25 litre (44 fl oz/5 cup) ovenproof dish with a little olive oil. Heat the remaining oil in a large saucepan and cook the leek over moderate heat until soft. Add the stock, thyme and potato. Cover and leave to simmer for 5 minutes.

Using tongs, lift half the potato out and place in ovenproof dish. Sprinkle with olives and parmesan; season with salt and freshly ground black pepper.

Layer with remaining potato. Spoon leek and stock mixture in at the side of the dish, keeping the top dry.

Scatter chopped butter over potato and bake, uncovered, for 50 minutes, or until cooked and golden brown. Leave in a warm place for 10 minutes before serving.

Serves 4–6

Note: Keeping the top layer of potato dry as you pour in the stock mixture will give the dish a crisp finish.

Cucumber, feta, mint and dill salad

125 g (4½ oz) feta cheese
4 Lebanese (short) cucumbers
1 small red onion, thinly sliced
1½ tablespoons finely chopped dill
1 tablespoon dried mint
3 tablespoons olive oil
1½ tablespoons lemon juice
crusty bread, to serve

Crumble the feta into 1 cm (½ inch) chunks and place in a large bowl. Cut the cucumbers into 1 cm (½ inch) lengths, then add to the bowl along with the onion and dill.

Grind mint in a mortar and pestle, or force it through a sieve until it is powdered. Tip into a small bowl, add olive oil and lemon juice and whisk until combined. Season with sea salt and freshly ground black pepper, pour over salad and toss well. Serve with crusty bread.

Serves 4

French shallot tarte Tatin

750 g (1 lb 10 oz) large brown
  shallots, unpeeled
50 g (1¾ oz) unsalted butter,
  plus extra, for greasing
2 tablespoons olive oil
4 tablespoons soft brown sugar
3 tablespoons balsamic vinegar

Pastry
125 g (4½ oz/1 cup) plain
  (all-purpose) flour
60 g (2¼ oz) cold unsalted butter,
  chopped
2 teaspoons wholegrain mustard
1 egg yolk, mixed with 1 tablespoon
  iced water

Cook shallots in a saucepan of boiling water for 5 minutes. Cool, then peel, leaving the root ends intact. Heat the butter and oil in a large heavy-based frying pan. Cook the shallots over low heat, stirring often, for 15 minutes, or until softened. Add the sugar, vinegar and 3 tablespoons water and stir to dissolve the sugar. Simmer, turning occasionally, for 15–20 minutes, or until liquid is reduced and syrupy.

To make the pastry, sift the flour and a pinch of salt into a bowl. Rub the butter and mustard into the flour until it resembles breadcrumbs. Make a well in the centre, add the egg yolk and mix until a dough forms. Gather together and press into a disc. Cover and chill for 30 minutes.

Preheat the oven to 200°C (400°F/ Gas 6). Grease a shallow 20 cm (8 inch) round tin. Pack the shallots in the tin and drizzle with any remaining syrup. Roll out pastry on a sheet of baking paper to a circle 1 cm (½ inch) larger than the tin. Lift into the tin and push down so it is slightly moulded over shallots. Bake for 20–25 minutes, or until golden. Stand tin on a wire rack for 5 minutes. Place a plate over the tin and turn out the tart. Gently invert onto a serving plate.

Serves 6

Aromatic vegetable and chickpea curry

1 tablespoon peanut oil
1 onion, chopped
2 garlic cloves, crushed
1½ teaspoons ground cumin
1 teaspoon ground turmeric
1½ teaspoons ground coriander
1 green chilli, deseeded and chopped
2 all-purpose potatoes, chopped into 4 cm (1½ inch) pieces
2 carrots, cut into 4 cm (1½ inch) pieces
400 g (14 oz) tinned chopped tomatoes
80 g (2¾ oz/½ cup) frozen peas
420 g (15 oz) tinned chickpeas, drained, rinsed
500 ml (17 fl oz/2 cups) vegetable stock
90 g (3¼ oz) baby English spinach leaves

Saffron and cardamom rice
500 ml (17 fl oz/2 cups) vegetable stock
6–8 saffron threads
6 cardamom pods
400 g (14 oz/2 cups) basmati rice

Heat oil in a saucepan over medium heat. Cook onion and garlic, stirring, for 3 minutes, or until the onion is transparent. Add the cumin, turmeric, coriander and chilli; stir until spices are fragrant. Add potatoes and carrots to pan. Cook 1 minute, stirring to coat in the spice mix. Stir in tomatoes, peas, chickpeas and vegetable stock, cover saucepan with a lid and cook for 20 minutes, stirring occasionally.

Stir in the spinach leaves and cook until the spinach is wilted. Season the curry with salt and pepper to taste.

To make the rice, bring the stock to the boil in a saucepan. Add saffron, cardamom and rice. Bring the water back to the boil, reduce the heat to low, cover with a lid and steam the rice for 20 minutes. Remove from the heat. Fluff with a fork and serve with the curry.

Serves 4

Potato omelette

500 g (1 lb 2 oz) all-purpose
  potatoes, peeled and cut into
  1 cm (½ inch) slices
60 ml (2 fl oz/¼ cup) olive oil
1 brown onion, thinly sliced
4 garlic cloves, thinly sliced
2 tablespoons finely chopped
  flat-leaf (Italian) parsley
6 eggs

Put potato slices in a large saucepan, cover with cold water and bring to the boil over high heat. Boil for 5 minutes, then drain and set aside.

Heat the oil in a deep-sided non-stick frying pan over medium heat. Add onion and garlic and cook 5 minutes, or until onion softens.

Add the potato and parsley to the pan and stir to combine. Cook over medium heat for 5 minutes, gently pressing down into the pan.

Whisk the eggs with 1 teaspoon each of salt and freshly ground black pepper and pour evenly over potato. Cover and cook over low–medium heat for 20 minutes, or until the eggs are just set. Slide onto a serving plate or serve directly from the pan.

Serves 6

Spinach pie

1.5 kg (3 lb 5 oz) English spinach
2 teaspoons olive oil
1 onion, chopped
4 spring onions (scallions), chopped
750 g (1 lb 10 oz/3 cups) low-fat
 cottage cheese
2 eggs, lightly beaten
2 garlic cloves, crushed
pinch of ground nutmeg
1 large handful mint, chopped
8 sheets filo pastry
30 g (1 oz) butter, melted
40 g (1½ oz/½ cup) fresh
 breadcrumbs

Preheat oven to 180°C (350°F/Gas 4). Lightly spray a 1.5 litre (52 fl oz/6 cup) capacity ovenproof dish with oil. Trim and wash the spinach, then place in a large saucepan. Cover and cook for 2–3 minutes, until the spinach has just wilted. Drain, cool then squeeze dry and chop.

Heat the oil in a small pan. Add the onion and spring onion, and cook for 2–3 minutes, until softened. Combine in a bowl with the chopped spinach. Stir in the cottage cheese, egg, garlic, nutmeg and mint. Season and mix together well.

Brush a sheet of filo pastry with a little butter. Fold in half widthways and line the base and sides of the dish. Repeat with three more sheets. Keep unused sheets moist by covering with a damp tea towel (dish towel).

Sprinkle breadcrumbs over the pastry. Spread the filling into the dish. Fold over any overlapping pastry and brush and fold another sheet and place on top. Repeat with three more sheets. Tuck pastry in at the sides. Brush the top with the remaining butter. Score diamonds on top using a sharp knife. Bake for 40 minutes, or until golden. Cut the pie into squares to serve.

Serves 6

Curried lentils

250 g (9 oz/1 cup) red lentils
500 ml (17 fl oz/2 cups) vegetable
 stock
½ teaspoon ground turmeric
50 g (1¾ oz) ghee
1 onion, chopped
2 garlic cloves, finely chopped
1 large green chilli, deseeded and
 finely chopped
2 teaspoons ground cumin
2 teaspoons ground coriander
2 tomatoes, chopped
125 ml (4 fl oz/½ cup) coconut milk

Rinse the lentils and drain well. Place
lentils, stock and turmeric in a large
heavy-based saucepan. Bring to the
boil, reduce the heat and simmer,
covered, for 10 minutes, or until just
tender. Stir occasionally and check
the mixture is not catching on the
bottom of the pan.

Heat ghee in a small frying pan and
add the onion. Cook until soft and
golden. Add garlic, chilli, cumin and
coriander. Cook, stirring, for about
3 minutes, until fragrant. Stir onions
and spices into lentil mixture and then
add tomato. Simmer over a very low
heat for 5 minutes, stirring frequently.

Season to taste and add the coconut
milk. Stir until heated through. Serve
with rice or naan bread.

Serves 4

Mushroom, ricotta and olive pizza

4 roma (plum) tomatoes, quartered
¾ teaspoon caster (superfine) sugar
10 g (¼ oz) dry yeast or 15 g (½ oz)
  fresh yeast
125 ml (4 fl oz/½ cup) skim milk
220 g (7¾ oz/1¾ cups) plain
  (all-purpose) flour
2 teaspoons olive oil
2 garlic cloves, crushed
1 onion, thinly sliced
750 g (1 lb 10 oz) mushrooms, sliced
250 g (9 oz/1 cup) low-fat ricotta
  cheese
2 tablespoons sliced black olives
small handful basil leaves

Preheat the oven to 210°C (415°F/ Gas 6–7). Put tomato on a baking tray lined with baking paper and sprinkle with salt, cracked black pepper and ½ teaspoon sugar. Bake 20 minutes, or until the edges start to darken.

Stir yeast and remaining sugar with 3 tablespoons warm water until yeast dissolves. Cover and leave in a warm place until foamy. Warm the milk. Sift flour into a large bowl and stir in the yeast and milk. Mix to a soft dough, turn onto a lightly floured surface and knead for 5 minutes. Leave, covered, in a lightly oiled bowl in a warm place for about 40 minutes, or until doubled in size.

Heat oil in a frying pan and fry the garlic and onion until soft. Add the mushrooms and stir until soft, and the liquid has evaporated. Leave to cool.

Turn the dough onto a lightly floured surface and knead lightly. Roll out to a 38 cm (15 inch) circle and transfer to a lightly greased oven tray. Spread with the ricotta, leaving a border. Top with mushrooms, tomato and olives. Fold the dough edge over onto the mushroom and dust the edge with flour. Bake for 25 minutes, or until the crust is golden. Garnish with basil.

Serves 6

Baked sweet potatoes with avocado and corn salsa

4 x 200 g (7 oz) orange sweet
  potatoes
1 red onion, finely chopped
1 avocado, finely chopped
1 tablespoon lemon juice
130 g (4½ oz) tin corn kernels,
  drained
½ red capsicum (pepper), finely
  chopped
1 tablespoon sweet chilli sauce
light sour cream or low-fat plain
  yoghurt, to serve

Preheat the oven to 200°C (400°F/
Gas 6). Prick the sweet potatoes a
few times with a skewer. Bake on
the oven rack for 40 minutes, or until
cooked through.

Meanwhile, place the onion, avocado,
lemon juice, corn and capsicum in a
bowl and mix together well. Stir in the
chilli sauce and season to taste with
salt and freshly ground black pepper.

Make a deep cut along the top of
each cooked sweet potato. Divide the
topping among the sweet potatoes
and add a dollop of light sour cream
or low-fat plain yoghurt, if you prefer.

Serves 4

Syrian burghul

2 tablespoons olive oil
1 large onion, finely chopped
½ teaspoon dried mint
175 g (6 oz/1 cup) coarse burghul
 (bulgur)
500 ml (17 fl oz/2 cups)
 vegetable stock
70 g (2½ oz/1 cup) finely sliced red
 cabbage
2 tablespoons chopped parsley
1 small handful mint, roughly torn
40 g (1½ oz/¼ cup) pitted kalamata
 olives, halved
½ lemon
½ pomegranate
200 g (7 oz/heaped ¾ cup) Greek-
 style yoghurt

Heat the oil in a large deep frying pan
with a tight-fitting lid over a medium
heat. Add the onion and dried mint,
and cook for 5 minutes, or until the
onion is soft. Stir in the bulgur until
coated, then add the stock. Cover
with the lid and steam over low heat
for 30 minutes. Do not remove the lid
during this time.

Stir with a fork, lifting up any crunchy
bits from the bottom of the pan. Add
cabbage, parsley, fresh mint and
olives. Finely grate the lemon zest and
add to pan, then squeeze in the lemon
juice. Holding the pomegranate over
pan to catch the juice, scoop seeds
into the pan. Squeeze the remaining
juice into the pan and discard any
white pith that may have dropped in.
Season with salt and freshly ground
black pepper and toss lightly. Serve
warm with the yoghurt.

Serves 4

Gratin of crepes with pumpkin, goat's cheese and crisp sage leaves

Crepes
310 ml (10¾ fl oz/1¼ cups) milk
50 g (1¾ oz) butter
155 g (5½ oz/1¼ cups) plain
  (all-purpose) flour
3 eggs
melted butter, for pan-frying

Filling
400 g (14 oz) butternut pumpkin
  (winter squash), peeled and cut into
  24 slices 1 cm (½ inch) thick
2 tablespoons olive oil
125 ml (4 fl oz/½ cup) vegetable oil
30 g (1 oz/1 bunch) sage, leaves
  plucked
250 g (9 oz) soft goat's cheese

300 ml (10½ fl oz) pouring cream
150 g (5½ oz) fontina cheese, grated

To make the crepes, gently heat the milk and butter in a small saucepan until combined. Put the flour and a pinch of salt in a large bowl and make a well in the centre. Add eggs and whisk in milk mixture until smooth. Stand for 10–15 minutes. Heat a non-stick frying pan over medium heat. Drizzle in some melted butter. Add 60 ml (2 fl oz/¼ cup) of the batter and swirl to cover the base. Cook for 30 seconds, or until bubbles appear. Turn; cook for 30 seconds. Transfer to a plate. You will need 12 crepes.

Heat a chargrill pan to medium. Put the pumpkin in a large bowl with the olive oil and toss with pepper to coat. Chargrill in batches for 1–2 minutes. Heat the vegetable oil in a small frying pan. Fry the sage leaves in batches until crisp, then drain on paper towels.

Heat oven grill (broiler) to its highest setting. Put 2 pumpkin slices, some goat's cheese and sage leaves in one quarter of each crepe, saving some sage leaves. Fold into triangles and divide among 4 ovenproof dishes. Heat the cream in a small saucepan, then stir in the grated cheese and pour over the crepes. Put dishes on a baking tray and cook for 3–5 minutes, or until cheese is bubbling. Sprinkle with sage leaves.

Serves 4

Chickpea burgers

2 teaspoons olive oil
1 small onion, finely chopped
2 garlic cloves, crushed
2 x 400 g (14 oz) tins chickpeas,
   rinsed and drained
95 g (3½ oz/½ cup) cooked brown
   rice
50 g (1¾ oz/⅓ cup) sun-dried
   tomatoes, chopped
1 eggplant (aubergine), cut into 1 cm
   (½ inch) slices
olive oil, for brushing
1 large red onion, sliced into rings
2 large handfuls rocket (arugula)
   leaves
6 pieces Turkish bread

Spicy yoghurt dressing
200 g (7 oz) thick plain yoghurt
1 garlic clove, crushed
¼ teaspoon ground cumin
¼ teaspoon ground coriander

Heat the oil in a frying pan and cook the onion for 2 minutes, or until soft. Add the garlic and cook for 1 minute. Cool slightly, then transfer to a food processor with the chickpeas, rice and sun-dried tomato. Process in short bursts until combined and the chickpeas are broken up. Season, then shape into six even patties about 8 cm (3 inches) in diameter. Place on a tray, lined with plastic wrap, cover and refrigerate for 1 hour.

Put the yoghurt dressing ingredients in a small bowl and mix well. Refrigerate.

Preheat a barbecue flat plate to moderately hot. Lightly brush the eggplant slices with oil, and toss a little oil through the onion rings. Cook eggplant and onion until tender and lightly golden. The eggplant will need about 3 minutes each side, the onion about 5 minutes. Transfer to a plate. Brush the chickpea patties lightly with oil and cook for 3 minutes. Turn and cook for a further 3 minutes, or until golden. They may stick a little, so make sure you get your spatula well underneath them before turning.

Arrange the rocket, eggplant and onion on the Turkish bread. Add the chickpea patties, some of the spicy yoghurt dressing and serve at once.

Makes 6

Mushroom quiche with parsley pastry

155 g (5½ oz/1¼ cups) plain (all-purpose) flour
3 tablespoons very finely chopped parsley
90 g (3¼ oz) cold unsalted butter, chopped
1 egg yolk, mixed with 2 tablespoons iced water

Mushroom filling
30 g (1 oz) unsalted butter
1 red onion, finely chopped
175 g (6 oz) button mushrooms, sliced
1 teaspoon lemon juice
4 tablespoons chopped parsley
3 tablespoons snipped chives
2 eggs, lightly beaten
170 ml (5½ fl oz/⅔ cup) pouring cream

Sift the flour and a pinch of salt into a large bowl. Stir in the parsley. Rub the butter into the flour until it resembles breadcrumbs. Make a well in the centre. Add the egg yolk mixture and mix using a flat-bladed knife until a dough forms, adding extra water if needed. Gather into a ball, cover and refrigerate for 30 minutes. Roll out pastry on a sheet of baking paper until large enough to fit a 35 x 10 cm (14 x 4 inch) loose-based tart tin. Ease the pastry into the tin and trim the edges. Refrigerate for a further 20 minutes.

Preheat the oven to 190°C (375°F/ Gas 5). Line the pastry with baking paper and spread with a layer of baking beads or dried beans. Bake for 15 minutes, then remove paper and baking beads and bake for a further 10 minutes, or until the pastry is dry. Reduce the oven temperature to 180°C (350°F/Gas 4).

To make the filling, melt the butter in a frying pan and sauté the onion for 5 minutes, or until softened. Add the mushrooms and sauté for 2 minutes, or until soft. Stir in the lemon juice and herbs. Meanwhile, mix the eggs and cream together and season. Spread the mushroom mixture into the pastry shell and pour in egg mixture. Bake for 25–30 minutes, or until set.

Serves 4–6

Chargrilled vegetable skewers with harissa and yoghurt

Harissa
2 teaspoons cumin seeds
½ teaspoon caraway seeds
75 g (2½ oz) large red chillies, chopped
3 garlic cloves, chopped
1 teaspoon sea salt flakes
50 g (1¾ oz) tomato paste (concentrated purée)
4 tablespoons olive oil

1 eggplant (aubergine), cut into 2 cm (¾ inch) cubes
150 g (5½ oz) button mushrooms, stems trimmed and sliced in half
250 g (9 oz) cherry tomatoes
1 zucchini (courgette), sliced
125 g (4½ oz/½ cup) Greek-style yoghurt
steamed rice and coriander (cilantro) leaves, to serve

Soak eight bamboo skewers in water for 20 minutes. Heat a small non-stick frying pan (skillet) over a medium–high heat and dry-fry cumin and caraway seeds for 30 seconds, or until fragrant. Place in a small food processor with the chillies, garlic, salt, 50 ml (1¾ fl oz) of water and tomato paste. Purée until almost smooth. Gradually add the olive oil and purée until combined.

Preheat a barbecue or chargrill plate to medium–high heat. Thread the eggplant, mushrooms, tomatoes and zucchini onto the skewers. Brush generously with half the harissa.

Cook the skewers for 5–7 minutes on each side, or until golden. Serve the skewers with the extra harissa, yoghurt, steamed rice and garnish with coriander, if desired.

Makes 8 skewers

Stir-fried tofu with orange and fresh pineapple

250 g (9 oz) firm tofu, cut into cubes
5 cm (2 inch) fresh ginger, grated
2 teaspoons finely grated orange zest
oil, for cooking
2 large onions, cut into thin wedges
3 garlic cloves, finely chopped
2 teaspoons soft brown sugar
2 teaspoons white vinegar
250 g (9 oz) fresh pineapple, cut into
 bite-sized pieces
1 tablespoon orange juice

Put the tofu, ginger, orange zest and some freshly ground black pepper in a non-metallic bowl. Stir, cover and refrigerate.

Heat the wok until very hot, add 1½ tablespoons of the oil and swirl it around to coat the side. Stir-fry the onion, garlic and brown sugar over medium heat for 2–3 minutes, or until the onion is soft and golden. Stir in the vinegar and cook for 2 minutes. Remove from the wok.

Reheat the wok and add pineapple and orange juice. Stir-fry for 3 minutes over high heat, or until the pineapple is just soft and golden. Stir in the onion mixture, remove from the wok, cover and set aside.

Reheat the wok until very hot and add 1½ tablespoons of the oil. Stir-fry the tofu in two batches, tossing regularly until it is lightly crisp and golden. Drain on paper towels.

Return the tofu and the pineapple mixture to the wok, and toss to heat through. Season well and serve.

Serves 4

Baked ricotta with ratatouille

1.5 kg (3 lb 5 oz) firm ricotta cheese, well drained
4 eggs, lightly beaten
3 garlic cloves, finely chopped
2 tablespoons chopped oregano
sea salt
80 ml (2½ fl oz/⅓ cup) extra virgin olive oil
300 g (10½ oz) eggplant (aubergine), cut into 1.5 cm (⅝ inch) pieces
3 capsicums (peppers) (a mixture of yellow, green and red), trimmed, seeded and cut into 1.5 cm (⅝ inch) pieces
400 g (14 oz) tin chopped tomatoes

Preheat the oven to 180°C (350°F/ Gas 4). Lightly grease a 22 cm (9 inch) spring-form cake tin. Combine ricotta, eggs, 1 finely chopped garlic clove and 1 tablespoon chopped oregano in a bowl, and season to taste with sea salt and freshly ground black pepper. Pour the ricotta mixture into the tin, then tap tin twice on a work surface to expel any air bubbles. Bake ricotta for 1 hour 30 minutes, or until firm and light golden. Cool in the pan on a wire rack, pressing down on the ricotta occasionally to remove air bubbles.

Meanwhile, heat 2 tablespoons of the oil in a frying pan, add eggplant and cook for 4–5 minutes, or until golden. Add capsicum and remaining garlic and cook for 5 minutes, until capsicum softens, adding an extra tablespoon of oil if necessary. Stir in tomato and remaining oregano and cook for 10–15 minutes, or until the mixture is reduced slightly and the vegetables are tender. Season well, to taste.

Remove the ricotta from the pan and cut into wedges. Serve ricotta wedges with some ratatouille on the side.

Serves 8–10

Borlotti bean moussaka

250 g (9 oz/1¼ cups) dried borlotti
  (cranberry) beans
2 large eggplants (aubergines), sliced
80 ml (2½ fl oz/⅓ cup) olive oil
1 onion, chopped
1 garlic clove, crushed
125 g (4½ oz) button mushrooms,
  wiped clean and sliced
250 ml (9 fl oz/1 cup) red wine
2 x 440 g (15½ oz) tins diced, peeled
  tomatoes
1 tablespoon tomato paste
  (concentrated purée)
1 tablespoon chopped oregano

Topping
500 ml (17 fl oz/2 cups) milk
250 g (9 oz/1 cup) plain yoghurt
4 eggs, lightly beaten
¼ teaspoon sweet paprika
50 g (1¾ oz/½ cup) grated parmesan
  cheese
40 g (1½ oz/½ cup) fresh
  breadcrumbs

Soak the borlotti beans in cold water overnight. Drain, rinse and transfer to a saucepan. Cover with water and bring to the boil. Reduce the heat to a simmer and cook over low heat for 1½ hours, or until tender. Drain well and spoon into a large ovenproof dish.

Preheat the oven grill (broiler) to medium–high. Sprinkle the eggplant with salt and stand for 30 minutes. Rinse, then pat dry. Brush with oil, then grill for 3 minutes on each side, or until golden. Drain on paper towels.

Preheat the oven to 200°C (400°F/ Gas 6). Heat the remaining oil in a large, heavy-based saucepan. Add the onion and garlic and cook over medium heat for 4–5 minutes, or until golden. Add the mushrooms and cook for 3 minutes, or until browned. Add the wine and cook over high heat for 2–3 minutes. Stir in the tomatoes, tomato paste and oregano. Bring to the boil, then simmer for 40 minutes, or until reduced and thickened. Spoon over the beans and top with eggplant.

To make the topping, whisk the milk, yoghurt, eggs and paprika. Pour over the eggplant. Stand for 10 minutes. Sprinkle with combined parmesan and breadcrumbs. Bake for 50 minutes, or until bubbling and golden.

Serves 6

Potato pizza

10 g (¼ oz) sachet dry yeast
310 g (11 oz/2½ cups) plain
  (all-purpose) flour
2 teaspoons polenta or semolina
2 tablespoons olive oil
2 garlic cloves, crushed
4–5 potatoes, unpeeled, thinly sliced
1 tablespoon rosemary leaves

Preheat the oven to 210°C (415°F/ Gas 6–7). Combine the yeast and ½ teaspoon each of salt and sugar with 250 ml (9 fl oz/1 cup) warm water in a bowl. Cover and leave in a warm place for 10 minutes, or until foamy. Sift the flour into a bowl, make a well in the centre, add the yeast mixture and mix to a dough.

Turn dough out onto a lightly floured surface and knead for 5 minutes, or until smooth and elastic. Roll out to a 30 cm (12 inch) circle. Lightly spray pizza tray with oil and sprinkle with the polenta or semolina.

Place the pizza base on the tray. Mix 2 teaspoons of the oil with the garlic and brush over the pizza base. Gently toss remaining olive oil, potato slices, rosemary leaves, 1 teaspoon of salt and some pepper in a bowl.

Arrange potato slices in overlapping circles over the pizza base and bake for 40 minutes, or until the base is crisp and golden.

Serves 6

Vegetarian chilli

130 g (4½ oz/¾ cup) burghul (bulgur)
2 tablespoons olive oil
1 large onion, finely chopped
2 garlic cloves, crushed
1 teaspoon chilli powder
2 teaspoons ground cumin
1 teaspoon cayenne pepper
½ teaspoon ground cinnamon
2 x 400 g (14 oz) tins chopped
  tomatoes
750 ml (26 fl oz/3 cups) vegetable
  stock
440 g (15½ oz) tin red kidney beans,
  drained and rinsed
2 x 300 g (10½ oz) tins chickpeas,
  drained and rinsed
310 g (11 oz) tin corn kernels, drained
2 tablespoons tomato paste
  (concentrated purée)
corn chips and sour cream, to serve

Soak burghul in 250 ml (9 fl oz/1 cup) hot water for 10 minutes. Heat the oil in a large heavy-based saucepan and cook the onion for 10 minutes, stirring often, until soft and golden.

Add the garlic, chilli, cumin, cayenne and cinnamon, and cook, stirring, for 1 minute.

Add the tomato, stock and burghul. Bring to the boil, simmer 10 minutes. Stir in beans, chickpeas, corn and tomato paste; simmer 20 minutes, stirring often. Serve with corn chips and sour cream.

Serves 6–8

Tempeh stir-fry

1 teaspoon sesame oil
1 tablespoon peanut oil
2 garlic cloves, crushed
1 tablespoon grated fresh ginger
1 red chilli, finely sliced
4 spring onions (scallions), sliced on
  the diagonal
300 g (10½ oz) tempeh, diced
500 g (1 lb 2 oz) baby bok choy (pak
  choy) leaves
800 g (1 lb 12 oz) Chinese broccoli,
  chopped
125 ml (4 fl oz/½ cup) mushroom
  oyster sauce
2 tablespoons rice vinegar
2 tablespoons coriander (cilantro)
  leaves
3 tablespoons toasted cashew nuts

Heat the oils in a wok over high heat, add the garlic, ginger, chilli and spring onion, and cook for 1–2 minutes, or until the onion is soft. Add the tempeh and cook 5 minutes, or until golden. Remove and keep warm.

Add half the greens and 1 tablespoon water to the wok and cook, covered, for 4 minutes, or until wilted. Remove and repeat with the remaining greens and more water.

Return the greens and tempeh to the wok, add the sauce and vinegar and warm through. Top with the coriander and cashew nuts. Serve with rice.

Serves 4

Falafel with rocket and tahini yoghurt dressing

Falafel
250 g (9 oz) dried chickpeas
1 onion, finely chopped
2 garlic cloves, crushed
5 large handfuls parsley
4 large handfuls coriander (cilantro) leaves
2 teaspoons ground coriander
1 teaspoon ground cumin
1/2 teaspoon baking powder

Tahini yoghurt dressing
3 tablespoons Greek-style yoghurt
1 tablespoon tahini paste
1 garlic clove, crushed
1 tablespoon lemon juice
3 tablespoons extra virgin olive oil

vegetable oil, for frying
125 g (41/2 oz) rocket (arugula) leaves, to serve

Put the dried chickpeas into a bowl and add enough cold water to cover them by about 12 cm (41/2 inches) and leave to soak overnight.

Drain the chickpeas well and transfer to a food processor. Process until coarsely ground. Add the remaining falafel ingredients and process until smooth and a vibrant green. Leave to infuse for 30 minutes.

To make the tahini dressing, put all the ingredients in a bowl and whisk together until smooth. Season to taste and set aside until required.

Using slightly wet hands, shape the falafel mixture into 24 ovals (each about the size of an egg). Heat 5 cm (2 inches) vegetable oil in a wok or deep saucepan and fry the falafel in batches for 2–3 minutes, or until dark brown. Drain on paper towel and keep warm in a low oven while cooking the remaining mixture.

Arrange the rocket leaves on serving plates, top with falafel and drizzle over the tahini dressing. Serve immediately.

Serves 4

Silverbeet parcels

500 ml (17 fl oz/2 cups) vegetable
  stock
1 tablespoon olive oil
1 onion, chopped
2 garlic cloves, crushed
1 red capsicum (pepper), chopped
250 g (9 oz) mushrooms, chopped
110 g (3¾ oz/½ cup) arborio rice
60 g (2¼ oz/1½ cups) low-fat
  cheddar cheese, grated
1 large handful shredded basil
6 large silverbeet (Swiss chard) leaves
2 x 400 g (14 oz) tins chopped
  tomatoes
1 tablespoon balsamic vinegar
1 teaspoon soft brown sugar

Heat stock in a saucepan to maintain at simmering point. Heat oil in a large saucepan, add the onion and garlic and cook until the onion has softened. Add the capsicum, mushrooms and rice and stir until well combined. Gradually add 125 ml (4 fl oz/½ cup) hot stock, stirring until the liquid has been absorbed. Continue to add the stock, a little at a time, until it has all been absorbed and the rice is tender. Remove from heat, add the cheese and basil, and season to taste.

Trim stalks from silverbeet and cook the leaves, a few at a time, in a large saucepan of boiling water for about 30 seconds, or until wilted. Drain on a tea towel (dish towel). Using a sharp knife, cut away any tough white veins from the centre of the leaves. Place a portion of mushroom filling in the centre of each leaf, fold in the sides and roll up carefully. Tie with string.

Put the tomato, balsamic vinegar and sugar in a large, deep non-stick frying pan and stir to combine. Add silverbeet parcels, cover and simmer for 10 minutes. Remove the string and serve with tomato sauce.

Serves 6

Frittata

200 g (7 oz) zucchini (courgettes),
   cubed
250 g (9 oz) pumpkin (winter squash),
   cubed
300 g (10½ oz) potato, cubed
100 g (3½ oz) broccoli florets
3 teaspoons oil
1 small onion, chopped
1 small red capsicum (pepper),
   chopped
2 tablespoons chopped parsley
3 eggs
2 egg whites

Steam the zucchini, pumpkin, potato and broccoli until tender.

Heat 2 teaspoons oil in a 23 cm (9 inch) diameter non-stick frying pan. Add onion and capsicum and cook for 3 minutes, or until tender. Combine in a bowl with the steamed vegetables and the parsley.

Brush the pan with the remaining oil. Return all the vegetables to the pan and spread out with a spatula to an even thickness. Beat the eggs and whites together and pour into the pan.

Cook over a medium heat until eggs are almost set, but still runny on top. Wrap the handle of the pan in foil to protect it and place under a hot grill (broiler) to brown the frittata top (pierce gently with a fork to make sure it is cooked through). Cut into wedges to serve.

Serves 6

Yellow vegetable curry

60 ml (2 fl oz/¼ cup) oil
1 onion, finely chopped
2 tablespoons Thai yellow curry paste
250 g (9 oz) potato, diced
200 g (7 oz) zucchini (courgettes),
   diced
150 g (5½ oz) red capsicum (pepper),
   diced
100 g (3½ oz) green beans, trimmed
50 g (1¾ oz) bamboo shoots,
   trimmed and sliced
250 ml (9 fl oz/1 cup) vegetable stock
400 ml (14 fl oz) tin coconut cream
Thai basil leaves, to garnish

Heat oil in a large saucepan, add the onion and cook over medium heat for 4–5 minutes, or until softened. Add the curry paste and cook, stirring, for 2 minutes, or until fragrant.

Add all the vegetables and cook, stirring, over high heat for 2 minutes. Pour in stock, reduce heat to medium and cook, covered, for 20 minutes, or until the vegetables are tender. Cook, uncovered, over high heat for 5–10 minutes, or until the sauce has reduced slightly.

Stir in coconut cream, and season with salt. Bring to the boil, stirring frequently, then reduce the heat and simmer for 5 minutes. Garnish with the Thai basil leaves.

Serves 6

Potato gnocchi with tomato sauce

500 g (1 lb 2 oz) floury potatoes, unpeeled
1 egg yolk
3 tablespoons grated parmesan cheese, plus extra, to serve
125 g (4½ oz/1 cup) plain (all-purpose) flour

Tomato sauce
425 g (15 oz) tin tomatoes, chopped
1 small onion, chopped
1 celery stalk, chopped
1 small carrot, chopped
1 tablespoon shredded basil
1 teaspoon chopped thyme
1 garlic clove, crushed
1 teaspoon caster (superfine) sugar

Steam or boil the potatoes until just tender. Drain and cool for 10 minutes before peeling and mashing. Measure 2 cups mashed potato into a large bowl, mix in the egg yolk, parmesan, ¼ teaspoon of salt and some black pepper. Slowly add flour until you have a slightly sticky dough. Knead for 5 minutes, adding more flour, if necessary, until you have a smooth dough. Divide into four portions and roll each on a lightly floured surface to form a rope about 2 cm (¾ inch) thick. Cut into 2.5 cm (1 inch) slices and shape into ovals. Press each oval into the palm of your hand against a floured fork, to flatten slightly and indent one side with a pattern. Place in a single layer on a baking tray and cover until ready to use.

To make tomato sauce, mix all the ingredients with salt and pepper in a saucepan. Bring to the boil, reduce the heat to low–medium and simmer for 30 minutes, stirring occasionally. Allow to cool, then process in a food processor or blender, until smooth. Reheat if necessary before serving.

Cook the gnocchi in batches in a large saucepan of boiling salted water for 2 minutes, or until they float to the surface. Drain. Serve tossed through the sauce, sprinkled with parmesan.

Serves 4

Zucchini patties

Cucumber and yoghurt salad
1 Lebanese (short) cucumber
sea salt, for sprinkling
250 g (9 oz/1 cup) Greek-style yoghurt
1 small garlic clove, crushed
1 tablespoon chopped dill
2 teaspoons white wine vinegar
ground white pepper, to taste

300 g (10 oz) zucchini (courgettes),
    grated
1 small onion, finely chopped
3 tablespoons self-raising flour
4 tablespoons grated kefalotyri or
    parmesan cheese
1 tablespoon chopped mint
2 teaspoons chopped flat-leaf (Italian)
    parsley
a pinch of ground nutmeg
3 tablespoons dry breadcrumbs
1 egg, lightly beaten
olive oil, for pan-frying
rocket (arugula) leaves, to serve
lemon wedges, to serve (optional)

To make the cucumber salad, chop cucumber into small pieces, place in a colander, sprinkle with sea salt and set aside in the sink or on a plate to drain for 15 minutes. Combine the yoghurt, garlic, dill and vinegar in a bowl. Add cucumber and season to taste with sea salt and ground white pepper. Cover and refrigerate.

Preheat the oven to 120°C (235°F/ Gas ½). Put zucchini and onion in a clean tea towel (dish towel), gather corners together and twist as tightly as possible to remove all the juices. Tip the zucchini and onion into a large bowl, then add flour, cheese, mint, parsley, nutmeg, breadcrumbs and egg. Season well with sea salt and freshly cracked black pepper, then mix with your hands to a stiff batter.

Heat 1 cm (½ inch) olive oil in a large heavy-based frying pan over a medium heat. When the oil is hot, drop 2 tablespoons of batter into the pan and press flat to make a thick patty. Fry several at a time for 2–3 minutes, or until well browned all over. Drain well on paper towels and place in the oven to keep warm while cooking the remaining patties. Serve hot with rocket leaves and the cucumber and yoghurt salad.

Serves 4 as a starter or side dish

Broccoli and ricotta soufflé

60 g (2¼ oz/1 cup) small broccoli
   florets
2 tablespoons olive oil
40 g (1½ oz) unsalted butter
1 onion, finely chopped
1 garlic clove, crushed
400 g (14 oz/scant 1⅔ cups) ricotta
   cheese
50 g (1¾ oz/½ cup) grated parmesan
   cheese
5 egg yolks, lightly beaten
a pinch of nutmeg
a pinch of cayenne pepper
5 egg whites
a pinch of cream of tartar
3 tablespoons dry breadcrumbs

Preheat the oven to 190°C (375°F/ Gas 5).

Cook the broccoli florets in boiling salted water for 4 minutes, then drain well and roughly chop.

Heat olive oil and butter in a frying pan. Add the onion and garlic and sauté over medium heat for 5 minutes, or until onion has softened. Transfer to a large bowl and add the broccoli, ricotta, parmesan, egg yolks, nutmeg and cayenne pepper. Season with sea salt and freshly ground black pepper. Mix well.

In a clean, dry bowl, whisk egg whites with the cream of tartar and a pinch of sea salt until stiff peaks form. Stir one-third of the beaten egg white into the broccoli mixture to loosen, then gently fold in the remaining egg white.

Grease a 1 litre (35 fl oz/4 cup) soufflé dish. Sprinkle with breadcrumbs, turn the dish to coat, then shake out the excess. Spoon broccoli mixture into the dish and bake for 35 minutes, or until puffed and golden brown, and serve immediately.

Serves 4

Spicy vegetable stew with dahl

Dhal
165 g (5³/₄ oz/³/₄ cup) yellow split peas
5 cm (2 inch) piece of fresh ginger, grated
2–3 garlic cloves, crushed
1 red chilli, seeded and chopped

3 tomatoes
2 tablespoons oil
1 teaspoon yellow mustard seeds
1 teaspoon cumin seeds
1 teaspoon ground cumin
¹/₂ teaspoon garam masala
1 red onion, cut into thin wedges
3 slender eggplants (aubergines), thickly sliced
2 carrots, thickly sliced
¹/₄ cauliflower, cut into florets
375 ml (13 fl oz/1¹/₂ cups) vegetable stock
2 small zucchini (courgettes), thickly sliced
90 g (3¹/₄ oz/¹/₂ cup) frozen peas
1 large handful coriander (cilantro) leaves

To make the dhal, put the split peas in a bowl, cover with water and soak for 2 hours. Drain. Place in a large saucepan with the ginger, garlic, chilli and 750 ml (26 fl oz/3 cups) water. Bring to the boil, reduce the heat and simmer for 45 minutes, or until soft.

Score a cross in the base of each tomato, plunge in boiling water for 30 seconds, then into cold water and peel the skin away from the cross. Cut in half and scoop out the seeds with a teaspoon. Chop tomato flesh.

Heat oil in a large saucepan. Cook the spices over a medium heat for 30 seconds, or until fragrant. Add the onion and cook for 2 minutes, or until the onion is soft. Stir in the tomato, eggplant, carrot and cauliflower.

Add dhal and stock, combine and simmer, covered, for 45 minutes, or until vegetables are tender. Stir occasionally. Add the zucchini and peas during the last 10 minutes of cooking. Stir in the coriander leaves and serve hot.

Serves 4–6

Curried eggplant stir-fry

2 tablespoons vegetable oil
$1/2$–1 long green chilli, finely sliced
4 red Asian shallots, chopped
2 garlic cloves, finely sliced
2 tablespoons rogan josh masala
  curry paste or mild curry paste
350 g (12 oz) slender eggplants
  (aubergines), cut on the diagonal
  into 1 cm ($1/2$ inch) slices
3 vine-riped tomatoes, each cut into
  8 wedges
70 g ($2 1/2$ oz/$1 1/2$ cups) baby English
  spinach leaves

Heat oil in a large wok and swirl to coat. Add green chilli, shallots and garlic and stir-fry over high heat for 1 minute. Stir in the curry paste and stir-fry for 1 minute.

Add eggplant and stir-fry 3 minutes, or until the eggplant has softened a little. Add the tomato and 125 ml (4 fl oz/$1/2$ cup) of water. Cover the wok and cook for 10 minutes, or until the eggplant is cooked, stirring occasionally. Stir in the spinach leaves and cook for 1 minute, or until wilted. Serve immediately.

Serves 4 as a side dish

Polenta pie

2 eggplants (aubergines), thickly sliced
330 ml (11¼ fl oz/1⅓ cups) vegetable
 stock
150 g (5½ oz/1 cup) fine polenta
60 g (2¼ oz/heaped ½ cup) finely
 grated parmesan cheese
1 tablespoon olive oil
1 large onion, chopped
2 garlic cloves, crushed
1 large red capsicum (pepper), diced
2 zucchini (courgettes), thickly sliced
150 g (5½ oz) button mushrooms,
 cut into quarters
400 g (14 oz) tin chopped tomatoes
3 teaspoons balsamic vinegar
olive oil, for brushing

Spread the eggplant in a single layer on a board and sprinkle with salt. Leave for 15 minutes, then rinse, pat dry and cut into cubes.

Line a 23 cm (9 inch) tin with foil. Pour stock and 330 ml (11¼ fl oz/1⅓ cups) water into a saucepan and bring to the boil. Add the polenta in a thin stream and stir over low heat for 5 minutes, or until the liquid is absorbed and the mixture comes away from the side of the pan. Remove from the heat and stir in the cheese until melted. Spread into the tin and smooth the surface. Refrigerate until set.

Preheat the oven to 200°C (400°F/ Gas 6). Heat the oil in a large lidded saucepan over medium heat. Cook the onion, stirring occasionally, for 3 minutes. Add the garlic and cook for a 1 minute. Add the eggplant, capsicum, zucchini, mushrooms and tomato. Bring to the boil, then reduce the heat, cover and simmer, stirring occasionally, for 20 minutes. Stir in the vinegar and season. Transfer to a 23 cm (9 inch) pie dish, piling it up slightly in the centre. Turn out the polenta, peel off the foil and cut into 12 wedges. Arrange in a single layer, over the vegetables. Brush lightly with olive oil and bake for 20 minutes, or until lightly brown and crisp.

Serves 6

Tofu with soy

2 tablespoons soy sauce
2 tablespoons kecap manis
1 teaspoon sesame oil
500 g (1 lb 2 oz) firm tofu, drained
1½ teaspoons fresh ginger, cut into
  thin matchsticks
3 spring onions (scallions), finely sliced
  on the diagonal
1 large handful coriander (cilantro)
  leaves, chopped
1–2 tablespoons fried shallots

Combine the soy sauce, kecap manis and sesame oil in a bowl. Cut the tofu in half widthways, then into triangles. Place on a heatproof plate and pour the sauce over the top. Marinate for 30 minutes, turning the tofu once. Sprinkle ginger over the tofu. Place the plate on a wire rack over a wok of boiling water and cover with a lid. Steam for 3–4 minutes, then sprinkle with the spring onion and coriander and steam for 3 minutes. Garnish with fried shallots and serve immediately.

Serves 4

Sweets

Bread and butter pudding

30 g (1 oz) butter, softened
8 slices white bread
2 tablespoons caster (superfine) sugar
2 teaspoons mixed (pumpkin pie) spice
90 g (3¼ oz/½ cup) pitted dried dates, chopped
3 eggs
2 tablespoons caster (superfine) sugar, extra
1 teaspoon grated lemon zest
250 ml (9 fl oz/1 cup) pouring cream, plus extra to serve
250 ml (9 fl oz/1 cup) milk
80 g (2¾ oz/¼ cup) apricot jam

Lightly grease a shallow baking dish. Lightly butter the bread and cut each slice into four triangles, leaving the crusts on. Combine the caster sugar and mixed spice in a small bowl. Arrange half the bread triangles over the dish, sprinkling with all the chopped dates and half the combined sugar and mixed spice. Arrange the remaining bread over the top and sprinkle on remaining sugar mixture.

Preheat the oven to 180°C (350°F/ Gas 4). Put a baking tin in the oven and half-fill it with hot water.

In a large bowl, whisk together the eggs, extra sugar and lemon zest. Put the cream and milk in a small saucepan and bring slowly to the boil. Immediately whisk into the egg mixture, then pour over the bread slices. Set aside for 20 minutes to allow the bread to absorb the liquid. Cover the pudding loosely with foil. Bake in the water bath for 15 minutes. Remove the foil and bake for a further 15 minutes, or until golden brown.

Warm the jam in a microwave or in a small saucepan. Use a pastry brush to coat the top of the pudding with the jam. Return to the oven for 5 minutes. Serve with cream.

Serves 4–6

Amaretti-stuffed peaches

6 ripe peaches
60 g (2¼ oz) amaretti biscuits,
  crushed
1 egg yolk
2 tablespoons caster (superfine)
  sugar, plus extra, for sprinkling
3 tablespoons ground almonds
2 teaspoons amaretto
3 tablespoons white wine
20 g (¾ oz) unsalted butter, chopped

Preheat the oven to 180°C (350°F/
Gas 4). Lightly grease a 30 x 25 cm
(12 x 10 inch) baking dish.

Cut each peach in half and remove the
stones; if the peaches are cling-stone,
carefully use a paring knife to cut
around and remove the stone. Using
a paring knife, scoop a little of the
flesh out from each peach to create a
slight cavity. Chop the scooped-out
flesh and place it in a small bowl with
the crushed biscuits, egg yolk, sugar,
ground almonds and amaretto. Mix
together well.

Spoon some of the stuffing mixture
into each peach, then place peaches
in baking dish, cut-side up. Sprinkle
with the wine and a little extra sugar.
Dot with butter. Bake for 20 minutes,
or until golden. Serve warm, with
cream or ice cream.

Serves 6

Variation: When in season, use ripe
apricots or nectarines for this recipe.

Ricotta crepes with orange sauce

85 g (3 oz/²/₃ cup) plain (all-purpose) flour
1 egg, lightly beaten
330 ml (11¼ fl oz/1⅓ cups) milk
butter, for greasing

Filling
3 tablespoons sultanas (golden raisins)
250 ml (9 fl oz/1 cup) orange juice
200 g (7 oz/heaped ¾ cup) ricotta cheese
1 teaspoon finely grated orange zest
¼ teaspoon natural vanilla extract

Orange sauce
50 g (1¾ oz) unsalted butter
3 tablespoons caster (superfine) sugar
1 tablespoon Grand Marnier

Sift the flour and a pinch of salt into a bowl and make a well in the centre. Combine the egg and milk, then add to the flour and whisk until smooth. Cover and stand for 30 minutes. Heat a 16 cm (6¼ inch) crepe or non-stick frying pan. Grease with butter, then pour 3 tablespoons of batter into the pan, swirling to coat the base. Cook over medium heat for 1–2 minutes, or until golden. Turn and cook for 30 seconds, then transfer to a plate. Repeat to make eight crepes.

Preheat the oven to 160°C (315°F/ Gas 2–3). For filling, soak sultanas in orange juice for 15 minutes. Drain sultanas, reserving the juice. Combine with ricotta, orange zest and vanilla. Place a large spoonful of filling at the edge of each crepe and fold in quarters. Divide crepes among four ovenproof plates. Bake 10 minutes.

Meanwhile, make the sauce. Melt the butter in a small pan over low heat. Add the sugar and reserved orange juice. Stir over medium heat without boiling until the sugar has dissolved. Bring to the boil, then reduce the heat and simmer for 10 minutes, or until reduced. Stir in the Grand Marnier and cool for 3–4 minutes. Pour over the warm crepes and serve immediately.

Serves 4

Sunken chocolate dessert cakes

1 tablespoon melted unsalted butter
115 g (4 oz/½ cup) caster (superfine) sugar, plus 1 tablespoon extra
150 g (5½ oz) dark chocolate, chopped
125 g (4½ oz) butter
3 eggs
30 g (1 oz/¼ cup) plain (all-purpose) flour
ice cream, to serve

Preheat the oven to 180°C (350°F/ Gas 4). Grease four 250 ml (9 fl oz/ 1 cup) ramekins with the melted butter and coat lightly with the extra sugar.

Put chocolate and butter in a small heatproof bowl. Sit the bowl over a small saucepan of simmering water, stirring frequently until the chocolate and butter have melted. Take care that the base of the bowl doesn't touch the water. Remove from heat.

Whisk the eggs and sugar in a bowl, using electric beaters, until pale and thick. Sift the flour onto the egg mixture, then whisk the flour into the mixture. Whisk in melted chocolate.

Divide batter between the prepared ramekins and place on a baking tray. Bake for 30–35 minutes, or until set and firm to touch. Allow to cool in the ramekins for 10 minutes before turning out onto serving plates. If the cakes are reluctant to come out, run a knife around the inside edge of the ramekins to loosen them. Alternatively, serve them in the ramekins, dusted with icing sugar. Serve warm with ice cream or whipped cream.

Serves 4

Banana and plum crumble

30 g (1 oz/¼ cup) plain (all-purpose)
   flour
50 g (1¾ oz/½ cup) rolled (porridge)
   oats
30 g (1 oz/½ cup) shredded coconut
45 g (1¾ oz/¼ cup) lightly packed
   soft brown sugar
finely grated zest from 1 lime
100 g (3½ oz) unsalted butter, cut into
   cubes
2 bananas, peeled and halved
   lengthways
4 plums, halved and stoned
60 ml (2 fl oz/¼ cup) lime juice

Preheat the oven to 180°C (350°F/
Gas 4). Combine the flour, rolled oats,
coconut, sugar and zest in a small
bowl. Add the butter and, using your
fingertips, rub the butter into the flour
mixture until crumbly.

Put bananas and plums in a 1.25 litre
(44 fl oz/5 cup) capacity ovenproof
dish and pour over the lime juice.
Toss to coat in the juice. Sprinkle the
crumble mixture evenly over the fruit.
Bake for 25–30 minutes, or until the
crumble is golden. Serve hot with ice
cream or whipped cream.

Serves 4–6

Carrot, spice and sour cream cake

310 g (11 oz/2½ cups) self-raising flour
2 teaspoons ground cinnamon
1 teaspoon ground nutmeg
150 g (5½ oz/¾ cup) dark brown sugar
200 g (7 oz/1⅓ cups) grated carrot
4 eggs
250 g (9 oz/1 cup) sour cream
250 ml (9 fl oz/1 cup) vegetable oil

Orange cream cheese icing
3 tablespoons cream cheese, softened
20 g (¾ oz) unsalted butter, softened
1 teaspoon grated orange zest
2 teaspoons orange juice
125 g (4½ oz/1 cup) icing (confectioners') sugar

Preheat oven to 160°C (315°F/Gas 2–3). Grease a deep 22 cm (8½ inch) round cake tin and line the base with baking paper.

Sift the flour, cinnamon and nutmeg into a large bowl, then stir in the sugar and carrot until well combined.

In a bowl, beat together eggs, sour cream and oil. Add to flour mixture and stir until well combined. Spoon batter into the cake tin and smooth the surface even. Bake for 1 hour, or until a skewer inserted in the centre of the cake comes out clean. Remove from the oven and allow to cool in the tin for 10 minutes, before turning out onto a wire rack to cool completely.

To make the orange cream cheese icing, beat the cream cheese, butter, orange zest and juice in a bowl using electric beaters until light and fluffy. Gradually add the icing sugar and beat until smooth. Spread icing over the top of the cooled cake. Cut into slices to serve.

Serves 8–10

Lemon and lime curds

4 eggs
2 egg yolks
175 g (6 oz/³/₄ cup) caster (superfine)
   sugar
100 ml (3¹/₂ fl oz) lemon juice
2¹/₂ tablespoons lime juice
finely grated zest of 2 limes
300 ml (10¹/₂ fl oz) pouring cream
boiling water, for steaming
baby meringues, to serve
thick (double/heavy) cream, to serve

Candied lemons
115 g (4 oz/¹/₂ cup) caster (superfine)
   sugar
1 lemon, finely sliced

Preheat the oven to 160°C (315°F/ Gas 2–3). Line a roasting tin with a tea towel (dish towel), place six 185 ml (6 fl oz/³/₄ cup) ramekins in the tin.

Combine the eggs, egg yolks and sugar in a large bowl and whisk until the sugar has dissolved and mixture is well combined. Stir in lemon and lime juice and lime zest. Add cream and mix well to combine. Pour the mixture into the ramekins, then pour enough boiling water into roasting tin to come halfway up the side of the ramekins. Bake for 30 minutes, or until just set. Remove from the tin and allow to cool. Refrigerate until cold.

Meanwhile, to make the candied lemons, put the sugar and 125 ml (4 fl oz/¹/₂ cup) of water in a saucepan over medium-high heat and stir until sugar has dissolved. Add the lemon slices and bring to the boil. Reduce heat to medium and simmer without stirring for 5–10 minutes, or until the syrup has reduced a little. Remove from the heat and allow to cool. Refrigerate until ready to serve.

Place a candied lemon slice on top of each curd and drizzle with some of the syrup. Serve with baby meringues and thick cream.

Makes 6

Queen of puddings

500 ml (17 fl oz/2 cups) milk
50 g (1¾ oz) unsalted butter
140 g (5 oz/1¾ cups) fresh
  breadcrumbs
115 g (4 oz/½ cup) caster (superfine)
  sugar, plus 1 tablespoon extra
finely grated zest from 1 orange
5 eggs, separated
210 g (7½ oz/⅔ cup) orange
  marmalade
1 teaspoon honey
whipped cream, to serve

Preheat oven to 180°C (350°F/Gas 4).
Lightly grease a 1.25 litre (44 fl oz/
5 cup) rectangular ovenproof dish.

Combine the milk and butter in a
small saucepan and heat over low
heat until butter has melted. Put the
breadcrumbs, the extra sugar and
orange zest in a large bowl. Stir in the
milk mixture; set aside for 10 minutes.

Lightly whisk the egg yolks, then stir
them into the breadcrumb mixture.
Spoon into the prepared dish, then
bake for 25–30 minutes, or until firm
to the touch.

Combine the marmalade and honey
in a saucepan and heat over low heat
until melted. Pour evenly over the
pudding. Whisk the egg whites in a
clean, dry bowl until stiff peaks form.
Gradually add sugar, whisking well,
until mixture is stiff and glossy and
the sugar has dissolved. Spoon the
meringue evenly over the top of the
pudding and bake for 12–15 minutes,
or until the meringue is golden. Serve
pudding warm with whipped cream.

Serves 6

Spiced glazed oranges

250 ml (9 fl oz/1 cup) orange juice,
  strained
2 tablespoons caster (superfine) sugar
4 star anise
2 cinnamon sticks, broken in half
4 oranges, peeled and cut into 1 cm
  (½ inch) slices
vanilla ice cream, to serve

Put the juice, sugar, star anise and cinnamon sticks in a deep-sided frying pan (skillet). Stir over low heat for 3 minutes, or until the sugar has dissolved. Bring to the boil, reduce heat and simmer for 3 minutes, or until the liquid becomes syrupy.

Add the orange slices and simmer for 7 minutes, or until the oranges have softened slightly and are well coated with the syrup. Serve oranges warm, drizzled with syrup and topped with a scoop of vanilla ice cream.

Serves 4

Citrus delicious

60 g (2¼ oz) unsalted butter, softened
170 g (6 oz/¾ cup) caster (superfine)
  sugar
3 eggs, separated
125 ml (4 fl oz/½ cup) citrus juice
250 ml (9 fl oz/1 cup) milk
60 g (2¼ oz/½ cup) self-raising flour
2 tablespoons finely grated citrus zest
ice cream, to serve

Preheat the oven to 180°C (350°F/
Gas 4). Grease a 1.25 litre (44 fl oz/
5 cup) capacity ovenproof dish.

Cream the butter and sugar in a bowl
using electric beaters until pale and
fluffy. Add the egg yolks one at a time,
beating well after each addition. Stir
in the citrus juice, milk, flour and zest,
combining well.

Whisk the egg whites in a clean, dry
bowl until stiff peaks form, then gently
fold into the batter. Spoon the mixture
into the dish. Put the dish in a large
roasting tin and pour in enough hot
water to come halfway up the side of
the dish. Bake for 40–45 minutes, or
until golden and puffed (cover with foil
if the top starts to brown too quickly).
Serve hot or warm with ice cream.

Serves 4–6

Caramelized apple mousse

50 g (1⅓ oz) unsalted butter
60 g 5½ fl oz/¼ cup) caster (superfine) sugar
170 ml (⅔ cup) thick (double/heavy) cream
500 g (1 lb 2 oz) green apples, peeled, cored and cut into thin wedges
2 eggs, separated

Place the butter and sugar in a frying pan and stir over a low heat until sugar has dissolved. Increase the heat to medium and cook until mixture turns deeply golden, stirring frequently. Add 2 tablespoons of the cream and stir to remelt the caramel.

Add apple wedges and cook, stirring frequently, over medium heat for 10–15 minutes, or until caramelized. Remove 8 apple wedges and set aside to use as garnish.

Blend remaining apples and caramel in a food processor until smooth. Transfer to a large bowl, then stir in the egg yolks and leave to cool.

Whisk the egg whites in a clean, dry bowl until soft peaks form, then fold into the cooled apple mixture. Whip remaining cream until firm peaks form and fold into apple mixture. Pour into a 750 ml (26 fl oz/3 cup) serving bowl or into four 185 ml (6 fl oz/¾ cup) individual serving moulds. Refrigerate for 3 hours, or until firm. Serve with reserved apple wedges.

Serves 4

Sweet grape flatbread

100 g (3½ oz/¾ cup) raisins
90 ml (3 fl oz) sweet marsala
150 ml (5 fl oz) warm milk
115 g (4 oz/½ cup) caster (superfine) sugar
2 teaspoons active dried yeast
300 g (10½ oz/scant 2½ cups) plain (all-purpose) flour, plus extra, for dusting
400 g (14 oz/2¼ cups) black seedless grapes

Put the raisins in a bowl and pour the marsala over. Set aside. Put the milk in a small bowl. Stir in 1 teaspoon of the sugar, sprinkle yeast over and set aside in a draught-free place for 10 minutes, or until foamy. Put the flour, 4 tablespoons of the sugar and a pinch of salt in a bowl and mix together. Add the yeast mixture and mix until a rough dough forms. Turn out onto a floured surface and knead for 6–8 minutes, or until smooth and elastic. Place in a large oiled bowl, turning to coat in oil. Cover. Leave to rise in a draught-free place for 1 hour, or until doubled in size.

Drain raisins and squeeze dry. Lightly dust a baking tray with flour. Deflate dough using a lightly floured fist, then divide in half. Shape each half into a disc 20 cm (8 inches) in diameter. Place one disc on the baking tray. Scatter half the grapes and half the raisins over the dough, then top with the second disc. Scatter the remaining grapes and raisins over the top. Cover with a tea towel (dish towel) and leave in a draught-free place for 1 hour, until doubled in size.

Preheat oven to 180°C (350°F/Gas 4). Sprinkle the dough with the remaining sugar and bake for 40–50 minutes, or until golden.

Serves 6–8

Orange and apricot rice cake

200 g (7 oz) dried apricots
115 g (4 oz/½ cup) caster (superfine)
  sugar
125 ml (4 fl oz/½ cup) sweet sherry
200 g (7 oz/1 cup) medium-grain rice
1 litre (35 fl oz/4 cups) milk
1 fresh bay leaf, bruised
2½ teaspoons finely grated orange
  zest
4 eggs, lightly beaten
170 g (6 oz/¾ cup) caster (superfine)
  sugar
200 g (7 oz) fresh ricotta cheese
1 teaspoon natural vanilla extract
60 g (2¼ oz/½ cup) slivered almonds
icing (confectioners') sugar, for
  dusting

Soak apricots in 625 ml (21½ fl oz/ 2½ cups) boiling water for 1 hour. Transfer to a saucepan with the sugar and sherry and slowly bring to the boil. Reduce heat; simmer for 20 minutes, or until the apricots are very soft and pulpy. Cool, then strain the apricots, reserving the syrup.

Put the rice, milk and bay leaf in a saucepan. Bring slowly to a simmer, cover and cook over medium-low heat, without stirring, for 15 minutes, or until the rice is tender and most of the liquid absorbed. Cover and stand for 20 minutes.

Preheat the oven to 170°C (325°F/ Gas 3). Grease a 20 cm (8 inch) round spring-form cake tin and line the base with baking paper. Wrap a piece of foil around the base and up the outside of the tin to seal it. Combine the zest, eggs, sugar, ricotta and vanilla in a bowl and stir until smooth. Add to the rice and stir until combined. Pour half the mixture into the tin. Arrange the apricots on top, pour in the remaining mixture and scatter over the almonds. Put the tin in a roasting tin and pour in enough boiling water to come halfway up the side of the cake tin. Bake for 50 minutes, or until firm in the centre. Cool in the tin. Dust with icing sugar and serve with the reserved syrup.

Serves 8

Strawberries with balsamic vinegar

750 g (1 lb 10 oz) ripe small
  strawberries
3 tablespoons caster (superfine) sugar
2 tablespoons good-quality balsamic
  vinegar
mascarpone cheese, to serve

Wipe the strawberries with a clean damp cloth and hull them. Cut any large strawberries in half lengthways.

Place the strawberries in a glass bowl, sprinkle the sugar over the top and toss gently to coat. Cover with plastic wrap and leave for 30 minutes to macerate. Sprinkle the vinegar over the strawberries, toss gently, then cover and refrigerate for 30 minutes.

Divide the strawberries among serving glasses, drizzle with syrup and serve with a dollop of mascarpone cheese.

Serves 4-6

Spiced baked apples

melted butter, for brushing
4 green apples
3 tablespoons raw (demerara) sugar
3 tablespoons chopped dried figs
3 tablespoons chopped dried apricots
3 tablespoons slivered almonds
1 tablespoon apricot jam
¼ teaspoon ground cardamom
¼ teaspoon ground cinnamon
30 g (1 oz) unsalted butter, chopped
whipped cream, custard or ice cream,
   to serve (optional)

Preheat the oven to 180°C (350°F/
Gas 4). Brush a square, deep baking
dish with melted butter.

Peel the apples and remove the cores.
Gently roll each apple in the sugar. In
a bowl, mix together the figs, apricots,
almonds, jam and spices.

Fill each apple with some of the fruit
mixture. Place the apples in the baking
dish and dot with pieces of butter.

Bake for 35–40 minutes, or until the
apples are tender. Serve warm with
whipped cream, custard or ice cream,
if desired.

Baked apples are best prepared and
cooked just before serving.

Serves 4

Farmhouse rhubarb pie

185 g (6½ oz/1½ cups) plain
  (all-purpose) flour
2 tablespoons icing (confectioners')
  sugar
125 g (4½ oz) cold unsalted butter,
  chopped
1 egg yolk, mixed with 1 tablespoon
  iced water

Filling
220 g (7¾ oz/1 cup) sugar, plus extra,
  for sprinkling
750 g (1 lb 10 oz/6 cups) chopped
  rhubarb
2 large apples, peeled, cored and
  chopped
2 teaspoons grated lemon zest
3 pieces of preserved ginger, sliced
ground cinnamon, for sprinkling
icing (confectioners') sugar, for
  dusting (optional)

Sift flour, icing sugar and a pinch of
sea salt into a large bowl. Using your
fingertips, lightly rub the butter into
the flour until the mixture resembles
coarse breadcrumbs. Make a well in
the centre. Add egg yolk mixture to
the well and mix using a flat-bladed
knife until a rough dough forms.
Gently gather the dough together,
transfer to a lightly floured surface,
then press into a round disc. Cover
with plastic wrap and refrigerate for
30 minutes, or until firm.

Meanwhile, preheat oven to 190°C
(375°F/Gas 5) and grease a 20 cm
(8 inch) pie plate. Roll the pastry out
to a 35 cm (14 inch) circle and ease it
into the pie plate, allowing the excess
to hang over the edge. Refrigerate
while preparing the filling.

In a saucepan, heat sugar and 125 ml
(4 fl oz/½ cup) water for 4–5 minutes,
or until syrupy. Add rhubarb, apple,
lemon zest and ginger. Cover and
gently simmer for 5 minutes, or until
the rhubarb is cooked but still holds
its shape. Drain off the liquid and
allow the rhubarb to cool. Spoon into
the pastry shell and sprinkle with the
cinnamon and a little extra sugar. Fold
overhanging pastry over the filling and
bake for 40 minutes, or until golden.

Serves 6

Crème caramel

250 ml (9 fl oz/1 cup) milk
250 ml (9 fl oz/1 cup) cream
375 g (13 oz/1½ cups) caster
  (superfine) sugar
1 teaspoon natural vanilla extract
4 eggs, lightly beaten
4 tablespoons caster (superfine)
  sugar, extra

Preheat the oven to 200°C (400°F/ Gas 6). Place the milk and cream in a saucepan and gradually bring to boiling point.

Put the sugar in a frying pan and cook over medium heat for 8–10 minutes. Stir occasionally as the sugar melts to form a golden toffee. The sugar may clump together—break up any lumps with a wooden spoon. Pour toffee into the base of six 125 ml (4 fl oz/½ cup) ramekins or ovenproof dishes. Take great care doing this as the toffee is very hot.

Combine the vanilla, eggs and extra sugar in a bowl. Remove the milk and cream from the heat and gradually add to the egg mixture, whisking well. Pour the custard mixture evenly over the toffee. Place the ramekins in a baking dish and pour in boiling water until it comes halfway up the sides of the dishes. Bake for 20 minutes, or until set. Use a flat-bladed knife to run around the edges of the dishes and carefully turn out the crème caramel onto a serving plate, toffee side up.

Serves 6

Note: When making toffee, watch it carefully as it will take a little while to start melting, but once it does, it will happen very quickly.

Sweet bruschetta

250 g (9 oz/1 punnet) strawberries
200 g (7 oz) ricotta cheese
1 tablespoon icing (confectioners')
  sugar, plus extra to serve
2 teaspoons Grand Marnier, or other
  orange-flavoured liqueur
30 g (1 oz/¼ cup) toasted slivered
  almonds
4 thick slices panettone, pandoro or
  brioche
2 tablespoons soft brown sugar

Heat the grill (broiler) to high. Reserve 4 small strawberries and chop the rest into 5 mm (¼ inch) cubes. Put them in a bowl with the ricotta, icing sugar, Grand Marnier and almonds, and gently combine.

Put the bread slices on the grill tray and grill (broil) for about 1 minute or until golden brown on top. Turn the slices over, spread the ricotta mixture over the top and sprinkle with the sugar. Grill for about 45 seconds, or until the sugar has melted and the surface bubbles and browns. Transfer to a serving plate and dust lightly with icing sugar. Sit a reserved strawberry on each slice and serve hot.

Serves 4

Tiramisu

5 eggs, separated
175 g (6 oz/³⁄₄ cup) caster (superfine)
 sugar
300 g (10¹⁄₂ oz/1¹⁄₃ cups) mascarpone
 cheese
250 ml (9 fl oz/1 cup) cold strong
 coffee
3 tablespoons Kahlúa or other coffee-
 flavoured liqueur
36 small savoiardi (lady fingers/sponge
 finger biscuits)
80 g (3 oz/²⁄₃ cup) finely grated dark
 chocolate

Using electric beaters, whisk the egg yolks with the sugar in a bowl until the mixture is thick and pale and leaves a ribbon trail when dropped from the beaters. Add the mascarpone and beat until smooth.

Using clean, dry beaters and bowl, whisk the egg whites until soft peaks form. Fold into mascarpone mixture.

Combine the coffee and liqueur in a shallow dish.

Dip enough biscuits to cover base of a 25 cm (10 inch) square dish into the coffee mixture, dipping each biscuit for 2–3 seconds; the biscuits should be well soaked but not breaking up.

Arrange biscuits snugly in the base of the dish. Spread half the mascarpone mixture over the biscuits, smoothing the surface. Dip more biscuits into the coffee mixture and use these to neatly cover the mascarpone layer. Top with the remaining mascarpone mixture, smoothing the surface. Cover the dish with plastic wrap and refrigerate for 3 hours or overnight, to allow the flavours to develop. Sprinkle with chocolate, then serve immediately.

Serves 6

Little jam-filled cakes

280 g (10 oz/2¼ cups) self-raising
  flour
170 g (6 oz/¾ cup) caster (superfine)
  sugar
250 ml (9 fl oz/1 cup) milk
2 eggs, lightly beaten
½ teaspoon natural vanilla extract
75 g (2½ oz) unsalted butter, melted
80 g (2¾ oz/¼ cup) strawberry jam
12 small strawberries, hulled
icing (confectioners') sugar, for
  dusting

Preheat the oven to 200°C (400°F/
Gas 6). Grease a twelve-hole standard
muffin tin.

Sift flour into a bowl, add the sugar
and stir to combine. Make a well in
the centre. Put the milk, eggs, vanilla
and butter in a bowl, whisking to
combine. Pour into the well and, using
a metal spoon, gradually fold the milk
mixture into the flour mixture until just
combined. Divide three-quarters of the
cake batter between the muffin holes.
Top each with 1 teaspoon of the jam
and cover with the remaining cake
batter. Gently press a strawberry into
the centre.

Bake for 20 minutes, or until light
golden. Cool in the tin for 5 minutes,
then turn out onto a wire rack to cool
completely. Dust with icing sugar.

The cakes are best served on the day
they are made.

Makes 12

Caramelized pineapple and ginger tarte Tatin

165 g (5¾ oz/1⅓ cups) plain (all-purpose) flour
1½ teaspoon ground ginger
85 g (3 oz) unsalted butter, cut into cubes
1 egg yolk
50 g (1¾ oz) glacé ginger, chopped
100 g (3½ oz) unsalted butter, extra
160 g (5¾ oz/scant ¾ cup) caster (superfine) sugar
1 pineapple, peeled, quartered lengthways, cored and cut into 5 mm (¼ inch) slices
thick (double/heavy) cream, to serve

Put the flour, ginger and butter in a food processor and process until the mixture resembles fine breadcrumbs. Add the egg yolk, glacé ginger and 2–3 tablespoons of water and pulse until mixture comes together. Turn out onto a lightly floured surface and bring together in a ball. Cover and refrigerate for 20 minutes.

Melt the extra butter in a 24 cm (9½ inch) ovenproof frying pan over low heat, add the sugar and stir until dissolved. Increase the heat to medium and cook, stirring, until the sugar starts to caramelize and turn golden brown (the mixture may go grainy then will go smooth). Reduce the heat to medium–low and add the pineapple slices. Cook for 15 minutes, or until the pineapple is tender and the caramel mixture is reduced and thickened slightly.

Preheat the oven to 180°C (350°F/ Gas 4). Roll out the pastry between two sheets of baking paper to a disc slightly larger than the top of the frying pan. Lay the pastry over the top of the pineapple and tuck the edges down the side of the pan. Cook in the preheated oven for 35–40 minutes, or until the pastry is golden. Turn the tart onto a large serving plate, cut into slices and serve with cream.

Serves 6–8

Bananas foster

2 tablespoons unsalted butter
4 firm, ripe bananas, sliced in half
  lengthways
2 tablespoons soft brown sugar
2 tablespoons rum
vanilla ice cream, to serve

Melt the butter in a large frying pan. Add the banana halves, in batches, if necessary, and briefly cook over medium–high heat, gently turning them to coat in butter.

Add the sugar and cook for 1 minute, or until the banana is caramelised.

Sprinkle with rum, then divide among serving bowls and serve with a scoop of vanilla ice cream.

Serves 4

Marble cake

1 vanilla bean or 1 teaspoon natural
  vanilla extract
185 g (6½ oz) unsalted butter,
  chopped
230 g (8 oz/1 cup) caster (superfine)
  sugar
3 eggs
280 g (10 oz/2¼ cups) self-raising
  flour
185 ml (6 fl oz/¾ cup) milk
2 tablespoons unsweetened cocoa
  powder
1½ tablespoons warm milk, extra

Preheat the oven to 200°C (400°F/
Gas 6). Lightly grease a 25 x 11 x
7.5 cm (10 x 4¼ x 3 inch) loaf tin and
line the base with baking paper.

If using the vanilla bean, split it down
the middle and scrape out the seeds.
Put the seeds (or vanilla extract) in a
bowl with the butter and sugar and,
using electric beaters, cream mixture
until pale and fluffy. Add the eggs
one at a time, beating well after each
addition. Sift the flour, then fold it into
the creamed mixture alternately with
the milk until combined. Divide mixture
in half and put the second half into
another bowl.

Combine the cocoa powder and
warm milk in a small bowl and stir
until smooth, then add to one half
of cake mixture, stirring to combine
well. Spoon the two mixtures into the
prepared tin in alternate spoonfuls.
Using a metal skewer, cut through the
mixture four times to create a marble
effect. Bake for 50–60 minutes, or
until a skewer inserted into the centre
of the cake comes out clean. Leave in
the tin for 5 minutes before turning out
onto a wire rack to cool.

This cake will keep, stored in an
airtight container, for 3–4 days. It is
also suitable to freeze.

Serves 6

Plum cobbler

750 g (1 lb 10 oz) plums, quartered,
  stones removed
4 tablespoons sugar
1 teaspoon natural vanilla extract
whipped cream, to serve (optional)

Topping
125 g (4½ oz/1 cup) self-raising flour
60 g (2¼ oz) cold unsalted butter,
  chopped
3 tablespoons soft brown sugar
3 tablespoons milk
1 tablespoon caster (superfine) sugar
icing (confectioners') sugar, for
  dusting

Preheat the oven to 200°C (400°F/
Gas 6). Put the plums, sugar and
2 tablespoons water in a saucepan
and bring to the boil, stirring until the
sugar has dissolved. Reduce the heat,
then cover and simmer for 2 minutes,
or until the plums are tender. Remove
the skins if you wish, then stir in the
vanilla. Spoon mixture into a 750 ml
(26 fl oz/3 cup) baking dish.

To make topping, sift the flour into
a large bowl. Using fingertips, lightly
rub in the butter until the mixture
resembles fine breadcrumbs. Stir in
brown sugar. Add 2 tablespoons of
the milk and mix using a flat-bladed
knife until a soft dough forms, adding
more milk if necessary. Turn out onto
a lightly floured surface and gather
together to form a smooth dough. Roll
out until 1 cm (½ inch) thick and cut
into rounds using a 4 cm (1½ inch)
cutter. Overlap the rounds around the
side of the baking dish, over the filling.
Lightly brush with the remaining milk
and sprinkle with the caster sugar.

Set dish on a baking tray and bake
for 30 minutes, or until the topping is
golden and cooked through. Serve hot
or at room temperature, dusted with
icing sugar.

Serves 6

Apple and strawberry crumble

800 g (1 lb 12 oz) tin apple pie fruit
1 tablespoon caster (superfine) sugar
250 g (9 oz/1 2/3 cups) strawberries, hulled and sliced
75 g (2 3/4 oz/3/4 cup) rolled (porridge) oats
60 g (2 1/4 oz/1/3 cup) soft brown sugar
85 g (3 oz/1/2 cup) whole-meal (whole-wheat) all-purpose (plain) flour
1 tablespoon pumpkin seeds (pepitas)
50 g (1 3/4 oz) cold butter, chopped
low-fat vanilla or strawberry yoghurt, to serve

Preheat the oven to 180°C (350°F/Gas 4). Place the apples in a 1.5 litre (52 fl oz/6 cup), deep 20 x 5 cm (8 x 2 inch) ovenproof dish. Sprinkle with the sugar and stir through the strawberries.

Combine rolled oats, sugar, flour and pumpkin seeds in a bowl. Rub in butter, using fingertips, until crumbly. Do not overmix. Spread evenly over apple. Bake for 15 minutes, or until golden brown. Serve with yoghurt.

Serves 4–6

Polenta fruit cake

150 g (5½ oz/1 cup) polenta
  (cornmeal)
60 g (2¼ oz) unsalted butter, chopped
115 g (4 oz/½ cup) caster (superfine)
  sugar
150 g (5½ oz) pitted dates, chopped
95 g (3¼ oz/½ cup) chopped dried
  apricots
a pinch of nutmeg
1½ teaspoons finely grated lemon
  zest
2 eggs, lightly beaten
125 g (4½ oz/1 cup) plain
  (all-purpose) flour, sifted
55 g (2 oz/⅓ cup) pine nuts
icing (confectioners') sugar, for
  dusting

Preheat oven to 180°C (350°F/Gas 4). Grease a 21 x 11 cm (8¼ x 4¼ inch) loaf (bar) tin and line the base with baking paper.

Bring 500 ml (17 fl oz/2 cups) water to the boil in a large saucepan. Gradually add the polenta and a pinch of salt, stirring constantly. Reduce the heat to medium, add butter and continue to stir for 1–2 minutes, or until mixture thickens and comes away from the side of the pan. Remove from heat. Allow to cool slightly. Add remaining ingredients, except pine nuts.

Spoon the mixture into the prepared tin, smoothing the surface with the back of a wet spoon. Sprinkle the pine nuts over the top and press gently onto the top of the cake. Bake for 40–45 minutes, or until firm and a skewer inserted into the centre of the cake comes out clean. Leave in the tin for 10 minutes, then turn out onto a wire rack to cool. Dust with icing sugar and serve.

Polenta fruit cake will keep, stored in an airtight container, for up to 3 days.

Serves 6–8

Sweet yoghurt plait

650 g (1 lb 7 oz/5¼ cups) white bread
  (strong) flour
1 tablespoon ground cinnamon
3 teaspoons (9 g) instant dried yeast
2 eggs, lightly beaten
250 g (9 oz/1 cup) Greek-style yoghurt
125 ml (4 fl oz/½ cup) lukewarm milk
90 g (3¼ oz/¼ cup) honey
60 g (2¼ oz) butter, chopped
100 g (3½ oz/½ cup) chopped dried
  figs
1 egg
2 tablespoons milk

Icing
375 g (13 oz/3 cups) icing
  (confectioners') sugar, sifted
80 ml (2½ fl oz/⅓ cup) lemon juice

Combine 600 g (1 lb 5 oz/4¾ cups) flour, cinnamon, yeast and 1 teaspoon salt in a large bowl and make a well in the centre. Combine the eggs, yoghurt, milk and honey, then pour into the well. Using a wooden spoon, stir until a dough forms, then turn onto a floured surface and knead for 10 minutes, or until smooth and elastic. Grease a large bowl with oil, then transfer the dough to the bowl, turning to coat in the oil. Cover and leave to rise in a draught-free place for 1½ hours, or until doubled in size. Knock back the dough, then turn out onto a floured surface. Cut into six portions, then roll each into 30 cm (12 inch) lengths. Plait three lengths of dough together, tucking the ends underneath. Repeat with the remaining dough. Transfer to a large, greased baking tray. Cover with a damp cloth and leave for 30 minutes, or until doubled in size. Preheat oven to 220°C (425°F/Gas 7). Combine egg and milk and brush over tops of loaves. Bake 10 minutes, reduce heat to 180°C (350°F/Gas 4) and bake for 20 minutes, or until bread is golden and sounds hollow when tapped.

To make the icing, combine the sugar, lemon juice and 2 tablespoons boiling water and stir until smooth. Drizzle over the cooled loaves.

Makes 2 loaves

Chocolate fudge puddings

150 g (5½ oz) unsalted butter
175 g (6 oz/¾ cup) caster (superfine)
  sugar
100 g (3½ oz) dark chocolate, melted
  and cooled (see Tip)
2 eggs
60 g (2¼ oz/½ cup) plain (all-purpose)
  flour
90 g (3¼ oz/¾ cup) self-raising flour
30 g (1 oz/¼ cup) unsweetened
  cocoa powder
1 teaspoon baking powder
125 ml (4 fl oz/½ cup) milk
whipped cream, to serve

Sauce
50 g (1¾ oz) unsalted butter, chopped
125 g (4½ oz) dark chocolate,
  chopped
125 ml (4 fl oz/½ cup) pouring cream
1 teaspoon natural vanilla extract

Preheat the oven to 180°C (350°F/
Gas 4). Lightly grease eight 250 ml
(9 fl oz/1 cup) ramekins or ovenproof
tea cups.

Using electric beaters, beat the butter
and sugar until light and creamy.
Add the melted chocolate, beating
well. Add the eggs one at a time,
beating well after each addition. Sift
together the flours, cocoa and baking
powder, then gently fold into the
chocolate mixture. Add the milk and
fold through. Half-fill the ramekins,
then cover with pieces of greased foil
and place in a large, deep roasting
tin. Pour in enough hot water to come
halfway up the side of the ramekins.
Bake for 35-40 minutes, or until a
skewer inserted into the centre of
each pudding comes out clean.

To make the sauce, combine the
butter, chocolate, cream and vanilla in
a saucepan and stir over low heat until
the butter and chocolate have melted.
Pour over the puddings and serve with
whipped cream.

Serves 8

Tip: To melt chocolate, cut it into
cubes and place in a heatproof bowl.
Sit bowl over a saucepan of simmering
water, making sure the water does not
touch the base, and stir with a metal
spoon until melted.

Upside-down banana cake

Banana topping
50 g (1³/₄ oz) unsalted butter, melted
60 g (2¹/₄ oz/¹/₃ cup) soft brown sugar
6 ripe large bananas, halved
    lengthways

125 g (4¹/₂ oz) unsalted butter,
    softened
230 g (8 oz/1¹/₄ cups) soft brown
    sugar
2 eggs
185 g (6¹/₂ oz/1¹/₂ cups) self-raising
    flour
1 teaspoon baking powder
2 large, very ripe bananas, mashed

Preheat the oven to 180°C (350°F/ Gas 4). Grease and line the base and sides of a 20 cm (8 inch) round cake tin with baking paper.

To prepare the banana topping, pour the melted butter over the base of the prepared tin and sprinkle with the sugar. Arrange the bananas, cut side down, in a single layer over the base of the tin.

Using electric beaters, cream the butter and sugar until light and fluffy. Add the eggs one at a time, beating well after each addition.

Sift flour and baking powder into a bowl. Using a large metal spoon, gently fold flour into the butter mixture with the mashed banana. Carefully spoon batter over the banana slices in the cake tin, smoothing over the surface. Bake for 45 minutes, or until a skewer inserted into the centre of the cake comes out clean. Remove from the oven and leave to cool in the tin for 5 minutes, before turning out onto a wire rack to cool completely.

Upside-down banana cake is best eaten the day it is made.

Serves 8

Index

Index

Index

Index

Index

Published in 2011 by Murdoch Books Pty Limited

Murdoch Books Australia
Pier 8/9, 23 Hickson Road
Millers Point NSW 2000
Phone: +61 (0)2 8220 2000
Fax: +61 (0)2 8220 2558
www.murdochbooks.com.au

Murdoch Books UK Limited
Erico House, 6th Floor
93–99 Upper Richmond Road
Putney, London SW15 2TG
Phone: +44 (0)20 8785 5995
Fax: +44 (0)20 8785 5985
www.murdochbooks.co.uk

Chief Executive: Juliet Rogers
Publishing Director: Chris Rennie

Publisher: Lynn Lewis
Senior Designer: Heather Menzies
Photography (cover): Stuart Scott
Stylist (cover): Louise Bickle
Editorial Coordinator: Liz Malcolm
Production: Joan Beal

National Library of Australia Cataloguing-in-Publication Data
Title: Budget
ISBN: 978-1-74196-994-8 (pbk.)
Series: Chunky series
Notes: Includes index.
Subjects: Low budget cookery.
Dewey Number: 641.552

Printed by 1010 Printing International.
PRINTED IN CHINA

Cover credits: White dinner plate, White Home. Red floral fabric and pink stripe fabric, No Chintz.
Yellow bowl, pale blue plate and saucer, Mud Australia. Yellow and pink Stripe fabric, Ici et la.

IMPORTANT: Those who might be at risk from the effects of salmonella poisoning (the elderly,
pregnant women, young children and those suffering from immune deficiency diseases)
should consult their doctor with any concerns about eating raw eggs.

OVEN GUIDE: You may find cooking times vary depending on the oven you are using. For fan-forced
ovens, as a general rule, set the oven temperature to 20°C (35°F) lower than indicated in the recipe.